A

SAINSBURY

# THE CHOCOLATE
# LOVER'S
## COOKBOOK

## PATRICIA LOUSADA

# CONTENTS

Published exclusively for J Sainsbury plc
Stamford House Stamford Street
London SE1 9LL
by Martin Books
Simon & Schuster Consumer Group
Fitzwilliam House 32 Trumpington Street
Cambridge CB2 1QY

ISBN 0 85941 771 9

First published 1987
Reprinted with new cover 1991
Text © Patricia Lousada 1987, 1991
Photographs and illustrations © J Sainsbury plc 1987, 19

Printed in Italy by Printer Trento

# THE AUTHOR

Lady Lousada was born in New York City. Her Italian mother was a singer and an inspired cook with a wide knowledge of Italian and French cuisine. Patricia was a member of the New York City Ballet and her fellow dancers' love of good food further involved her in cooking. She later lived in Paris for two years, where the experience of attending lectures at the Cordon Bleu school, against a background of Parisian restaurants, deepened her interest still more. She has given lectures and demonstrations on various kinds of cooking.

Patricia has written a number of cookery books, the latest being *'Easy to Entertain'*. *'The Chocolate Lover's Cookbook'* is the fifth book she has written exclusively for Sainsbury's; her earlier titles include *'Pasta Italian Style'* and *'The Great American Bake-In'*. Lady Lousada lives in London with her English husband and has four children.

# INTRODUCTION

Chocolate is made from the bean of the cacao tree, which is native to the tropical areas of Central and South America. Thousands of years before the Europeans discovered it, the Mayans and Incas were brewing it as a drink, offering it to their gods during tribal ritual, and using it as currency between individuals and states.

*Techniques of Chocolate Preparation*

Although Columbus returned from the New World in 1502 bearing cocoa beans for the King of Spain, no one showed much interest in them. Twenty years later, Cortez again brought cocoa to Spain. He had first tasted it at the Mexican court of Montezuma in a cold, bitter drink called *chocolatl*, and he then planted cocoa beans in Africa on his way back to Spain. The Spaniards added vanilla and sugar to the spicy concoction he offered them, improving it so much that for nearly a century they jealously guarded the secrets of its cultivation and preparation from the rest of Europe.

But the monopoly on drinking chocolate couldn't last forever. Both Italian and English travellers in South America encountered it; Spanish Jews fleeing the Inquisition brought it into France, and it trickled into court life through the intermarriage of royal families. When it appeared in England in the middle of the seventeenth century, chocolate houses became important meeting places for the fashionable and well-to-do. Samuel Pepys writes in his Diary of enjoying *jocalatte*, and poets and playwrights, like Addison and Steele, mention the chocolate houses in their works.

The Cocoa Tree, and White's, which later became the first gentlemen's club in London, were among the most popular of these social centres, but only the wealthy gathered in them. The drink was an expensive luxury, so heavily taxed by the government that cocoa beans were often smuggled into the country. When Gladstone lowered the chocolate tax in 1853, prices fell and even the less affluent could enjoy drinking it.

They could also – for the first time – eat it. In 1828 Coenrad J. van Houten invented a press to extract cocoa butter from the bean, and in 1847 Joseph Fry, in Bristol, added chocolate liquor and sugar to this butter and made the first eating chocolate. The names of these pioneers of chocolate manufacturing are still in the forefront of the trade, as are those of Cadbury, who opened a shop in Birmingham in 1824, and Rowntree, who acquired a business in York in 1862.

As the world's appetite for chocolate increased – and it is still increasing today – manufacturing methods improved to meet the growing demand. Turning cocoa beans into edible chocolate is a long and complicated process which begins on the plantations, always located within twenty degrees of the equator. Cacao trees start producing when they are three to five years old. The beans grow in spindle-shaped pods which only form on the trunk and thickest branches of the tree. The pods are harvested twice a year and split open at once with a machete, so the beans can be scooped out and left to dry in the sun. An average tree only yields one or two pounds of dried beans a year, since the beans lose 50 per cent of their weight while drying.

Every manufacturer processes his own beans and each one uses his own special formula. The overall process, however, is the same throughout the world. The beans are roasted to bring out their flavour and then cracked so their protective shells and husks can be removed, leaving the kernels, called nibs. Once these are exposed they must be ground. The friction of the grinding melts the cocoa butter in the nibs, which accounts for 50 per cent of their make-up, and extracts most of it, leaving a thick paste called 'chocolate liquor'. This liquor, cooled and hardened, is unsweetened cooking chocolate. If the liquor is then pressed, more cocoa butter will be released from it, and the remaining hard mass, ground to powder, becomes cocoa.

All chocolate liquor retains some of its original cocoa butter content. To form sweetened chocolate, extra cocoa butter is added to the liquor, along with sugar and flavouring. Milk chocolate, now made with dried milk, was originally created in 1875, using condensed milk.

We owe the taste and texture of chocolate as we know it now to a Swiss manufacturer named Rodolphe Lindt. Until 1880, all eating chocolate had a rough, grainy texture. In that year Lindt increased the amount of cocoa butter in his chocolate recipe and mixed the enriched liquor repeatedly over several days, a longer period than was customary. The result of his innovations is the smooth, melting chocolate so popular today.

Chocolate is an obsession with some people and irresistible to most of us. The botanical name for the chocolate plant, *Theobrama cacao*, means 'food of the gods', but ordinary mortals seem to have been addicted to chocolate forever. Mexicans dip chicken in it, Sicilians add white onions to it and pour it over game birds, Italians created chocolate tagliatelli, and the most famous Austrian cake, Sacher Torte, wouldn't exist without it. The Americans have even devoted monthly newsletters to it, printed with chocolate-scented ink. Perhaps they know that Madame de Pompadour recommended chocolate as an aphrodisiac.

Although Madame de Sévigné predicted its fall from fashion in 1671, every year on average every American eats 10 lb of chocolate, every Englishman 16½ lb, and every Swiss citizen a staggering 22 lb.

When we want to make a dessert to please, we immediately think of chocolate. This book is packed with chocolate treats for many different occasions. It contains favourites such as Chocolate Velvet Mousse (page 14), Chocolate Cheesecake (page 63) and Bitter Chocolate Soufflé (page 51), as well as newer desserts and old-fashioned puddings. The book is full of ideas that will dazzle chocolate lovers: scrumptious cakes for special parties like birthdays or holiday gatherings, biscuits and small cakes for tea-time that are also delicious with coffee, and delectable ice creams for hot summer afternoons.

Chocolate desserts are elegant to look at and delicious to eat. Many are included here: the rich but light Three-Chocolate Terrine (page 18) can be surrounded by a contrasting fruit or cream sauce, and White Chocolate Ice Cream (page 44) served with kirsch-soaked cherries makes a striking finale to any dinner party. And practically every recipe can be prepared well in advance: what a treat for the cook!

## Vanilla sugar and vanilla essence

Some of the recipes in this book call for vanilla sugar. This is made by storing two vanilla pods in a jar of caster or granulated sugar. The jar can be topped up with more sugar for some time as the pods have quite a long life.

A few recipes call for vanilla essence. In the United States, pure vanilla extract is widely used in baking, but it is expensive and hard to find in this country. The artificial vanilla flavouring which is sometimes called vanilla essence here will impart a different flavour and should not be used as a substitute.

## Selection of chocolate for cooking

The quality of the chocolate used in cooking is all-important. You cannot expect to have good results with inferior chocolate. Use good plain chocolate that contains a minimum of 50 per cent cocoa solids. Buy plain cooking or baking chocolate or bitter or plain dessert chocolate. Sainsbury's now have a deluxe cooking chocolate with 51 per cent cocoa solids. Price is also an indication of quality. Buy the best you can afford. The cheaper brands, including 'chocolate-flavoured' coverings, have very little cocoa solids or butter and a high percentage of animal fats and synthetic flavourings and so are not suitable.

## Types of chocolate

**White chocolate** is made with cocoa butter, milk and sugar. It does not contain chocolate liquor and does not have a real chocolate flavour. It is often used in desserts to provide a contrast with dark chocolate.

**Milk chocolate** has a milder flavour than plain chocolate because of its milk content. It is not suitable for cooking but can be used as a decorative piping.

**Chocolate-flavoured cake covering** is unsuitable in flavour and texture for recipes in this book. Happier results can be achieved for coating and dipping by using plain chocolate and adding a small amount of oil, about 1 tablespoon for every 250 g (8 oz) of chocolate.

*Couverture* is a confectioner's chocolate used for coating purposes. It is hard to obtain and must be tempered to stabilize its high cocoa butter content before it can be used. This involves heating it to 43°C/110°F, cooling it to 26°C/80°F and reheating to about 40°C/90°F for coating.

**Cocoa powder** is the cheapest way of obtaining a chocolate flavour in cooking and can replace chocolate if necessary. Use 3 tablespoons of cocoa, 15 g (½ oz) of butter and 1 tablespoon of sugar for every 25 g (1 oz) of chocolate required. Drinking chocolate should not be substituted because it is too sweet.

## Melting chocolate

- Never melt chocolate over direct heat. The flavour will be impaired and it will 'seize' – go hard and grainy – if it becomes too hot.
- Butter or oil can safely be added to chocolate before or after it is melted without any risk.
- Chocolate can be added to a large quantity of hot liquid without any risk.
- Chocolate can also be safely melted with a small quantity of liquid. If you add a small amount of liquid to melted chocolate, however, the chocolate will seize. If this should happen you may be able to retrieve it by adding a little oil.
- Chocolate melts more evenly and quickly if it is broken or cut into small pieces. It should never be heated to a temperature greater than 44°C/110°F.

**Double saucepan method:** boil a small amount of water in the bottom of a double saucepan. The bottom of the upper pan should not touch the water and should fit tightly to keep the steam from coming in contact with the chocolate. Take the pan off the heat, add the chopped chocolate, cover and leave it until the chocolate has melted.

**Microwave-oven method:** place chopped chocolate in a microwave-proof cup or bowl and microwave on full power for 2½ minutes on a 650 watt oven. Check your manufacturer's booklet if your model has a different output.

**Oven method:** place chopped chocolate on a plate in an oven preheated to Gas Mark ¼ / 100°C/225°F for five minutes.

# Decorating with chocolate

For dipping or coating use a good plain chocolate and add 1 tablespoon of sunflower or groundnut oil to every 250 g (8 oz) of chocolate.

**Chocolate cups:** set several paper cake cases inside each other to help keep the shape of the inside cup you are going to coat. Spoon some melted chocolate that has cooled to blood heat or just below into the cup and make an even layer using a brush or small spoon. Make a second layer when set if it looks too thin. Keep refrigerated until ready to use. The chocolate shrinks as it cools and the paper can be peeled off. If you want a slightly wider cup splay the edges before coating. Make a few more than you need as a few are bound to break!

**Chocolate shells:** cover small, well scrubbed scallop shells as smoothly as possible with cling film. Melt 40 g (1½ oz) chocolate per shell (page 10) and brush an even layer over them. Leave to set for 30 minutes and then chill for a further 30 minutes. Make a few more than you need in case some of them break.

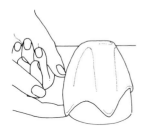

**Chocolate baskets:** to make four baskets, melt 175 g (6 oz) of chocolate with 1 teaspoon of oil in the top of a double saucepan. Place two layers of white tissue paper (not paper tissues) approximately 36 cm (14 inches) square on a flat surface. Using a spatula, spread the chocolate in a thin layer over the paper leaving a 2.5 cm (1-inch) border around the edge. Use the border to hold down the paper while you spread the chocolate. When the chocolate is slightly set but still warm, cut the chocolate into approximately four 15 cm (6-inch) squares. Discard the extra bottom paper and drape each chocolate-covered paper square over an upturned glass to make a fluted basket. The tissue paper lets the chocolate drape beautifully. Leave the baskets to set for 30 minutes and then refrigerate for another 30 minutes before you remove the paper. Always make a few more baskets than you need in case one breaks. With practice, you can make them elegantly thin. Ice cream looks particularly nice.

**Piping chocolate:** pour melted chocolate into a baking parchment piping bag and leave for a few seconds to cool and thicken. Cut a tiny hole in the tip of the bag, squeeze gently and pipe out designs or words or drizzle the chocolate over the surface to decorate.

**Cut-out shapes:** Line a baking tray with baking parchment. Melt plain chocolate and pour in just enough to cover the bottom of the tin. Smooth with a spatula and leave to cool, about 30 minutes. Reverse it on to a sheet of baking parchment and peel away the first paper. Using a long sharp knife or shaped cutters, cut the chocolate into shapes. Do not allow it to set too firmly before cutting or it may splinter.

**Chocolate leaves:** pick fresh leaves with distinct veins – holly and rose leaves work well. Coat the underside of each leaf with melted chocolate using a small brush, or by carefully dipping the leaf in the chocolate. Leave the leaf chocolate-side up to set. Peel the leaf away from the chocolate. Artichoke leaves are excellent for making large roses to decorate cake tops.

**Chocolate curls:** melt some chocolate and pour it on to a flat hard surface such as a marble slab or baking sheet. Quickly spread the chocolate with a palette knife to make a smooth, thin layer. Using both hands push a sharp knife along the surface at a 45° angle. If the scrolls break up try heating the knife in hot water and drying it before using. Make the curls before the chocolate sets hard. A tablespoon of light oil added to every 250 g (8 oz) chocolate makes it easier.

**Grated chocolate:** chill the chocolate before using and use an ordinary grater or rotary hand grater. Work over a large piece of baking parchment to catch all the bits.

**Dipped nuts and fruit:** almonds, walnuts and other nuts can be dipped on a fork. Tap the fork on the edge of the pan to drain off excess chocolate and place the nuts on baking parchment to set. It helps if the chocolate is at 40–42°C/90–95°F before coating. Soft or dried fruit can be dipped in the same way.

# COLD DESSERTS

## CHOCOLATE BAVARIAN CREAM

Preparation and cooking time: 35 minutes        Serves 10
+ chilling overnight

1½ tablespoons gelatine

125 ml (4 fl oz) cold strong coffee

350 ml (12 fl oz) milk

5 eggs, separated

150 g (5 oz) vanilla caster sugar (page 8)

2 tablespoons cocoa powder

100 g (3½ oz) plain or bitter chocolate, chopped finely

150 ml (5 fl oz) double cream, lightly whipped

2 tablespoons rum, Cognac or orange liqueur

a pinch of salt

**To serve:**

5 kiwifruit or 2–3 large navel oranges (optional)

*An elegant unmoulded dessert with a beautiful mousse-like texture. It looks wonderful made in a ring mould and decorated with kiwifruit or orange slices.*

Place the gelatine with the coffee in a cup and leave for 5 minutes until it is spongy. Place the cup in hot water and leave the gelatine to dissolve. Bring the milk to boiling point in a large saucepan. Meanwhile whisk the egg yolks with 125 g (4 oz) of the sugar and the cocoa. Pour the boiling milk over the egg mixture, whisking continually, and return to the saucepan. Stir constantly with a wooden spoon until the mixture begins to thicken and just coats the spoon. Do not allow it to boil or it will curdle. Remove the custard from the heat and stir in the gelatine all at once and then stir in the chocolate.

Whisk the egg whites with a pinch of salt until just stiff, add the remaining sugar, and whip until the whites are thick and glossy. Fold them into the hot chocolate custard. Place the bowl in iced water and fold the mixture occasionally while it thickens. When it starts to set, fold in the whipped cream and alcohol.

Rinse a 1.75-litre (3-pint) metal ring mould with cold water and shake out the excess. Pour in the mixture, cover it with cling film and refrigerate for at least 3 hours or overnight.

To serve: dip the mould in very hot water for a few seconds. Slip a knife around the edge and reverse it on to a serving plate, giving it a good shake to release it if necessary. Peel the fruit and cut into thin slices and arrange them over the top if used.

# CHOCOLATE VELVET MOUSSE

Preparation time: 35 minutes + 4 hours chilling                    Serves 6

150 g (5 oz) bitter or plain chocolate

3 egg yolks

65 g (2½ oz) unsalted butter, cut into small pieces

1 tablespoon crème de cacao, Tia Maria or liqueur of your choice

4 egg whites

3 tablespoons vanilla caster sugar (page 8)

a pinch of salt

### For the Crème Anglaise:

½ vanilla pod

300 ml (½ pint) milk

3 egg yolks

50 g (2 oz) vanilla caster sugar

*For a new approach to an old favourite, serve scoops of this velvety dark mousse on a luscious sea of Crème Anglaise.*

Melt the chocolate (page 10). Remove from the heat and beat in the egg yolks, one at a time. Stir in the butter and when the mixture is smooth, add the alcohol. Whisk the egg whites with a pinch of salt until they are thick; add the sugar and continue to whisk until the whites form stiff peaks. Using a large metal spoon fold a dollop of the whites into the chocolate mixture to lighten it and then fold in the remaining whites, incorporating as much air as possible. Turn the mixture into a 20 cm (8-inch) dish. Cover with cling film and refrigerate until set, about 4 hours.

To make the Crème Anglaise: split the vanilla pod in half lengthways and scrape the black seeds into a small saucepan. Add the scraped pods and milk and heat to just below boiling point. Beat the egg yolks with the sugar until pale and light and whisk in the hot milk. Pour the mixture into the saucepan and stir constantly over a very low heat until the mixture thickens slightly. Do not allow it to come near the boil or it will curdle. Strain the sauce into a bowl; don't worry if a few seeds remain. The sauce will thicken a little more as it cools. Keep the sauce refrigerated until it is needed.

To serve: pour some sauce on to individual plates. Dip a serving spoon in hot water and then dip the spoon into the mousse to make an oval-shaped scoop. Place the scoop round-side up on the Crème Anglaise.

*Chocolate Mille-feuille:* for this French variation, spread a very thin layer of melted chocolate over baking parchment and cut into rectangles approximately 6 cm (2½ inches) by 10 cm (4 inches) before the chocolate is hard. Allow about 4–5 per serving. Spread the mousse between the thin chocolate rectangles, stacking them up as you would a layer cake. Serve them on a bed of Crème Anglaise or Pistachio Sauce (page 92).

# MONT BLANC

Preparation and cooking time: 1 hour                    Serves 6

500 g (1 lb) chestnuts or 450 g (15 oz) can of chestnut purée (purée de marrons)

250 ml (8 fl oz) milk if using fresh chestnuts

6 tablespoons of double cream if using canned chestnut purée

50 g (2 oz) vanilla caster sugar plus 1 teaspoon (page 8)

150 ml (5 fl oz) double cream

1 tablespoon rum or brandy

50 g (2 oz) plain chocolate, refrigerated

a pinch of salt, if using fresh chestnuts

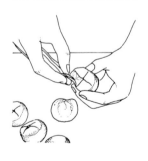

*In this dessert sweetened chestnut purée is piled mountain-high and topped with whipped cream and grated chocolate. If you have the patience to peel fresh chestnuts you will be rewarded by exceptionally good flavour but a can of chestnut purée lets you whip up a quicker version.*

If using fresh chestnuts bring a large pan of water to the boil. Cut a 'cross' on the flat side of each chestnut. Drop half the chestnuts into the boiling water and boil for 5 minutes. Remove a few at a time and peel off both the shells and the inner skins. Keep the rest in simmering water until ready to peel. Repeat with the remaining chestnuts. Put the peeled chestnuts in a saucepan with the milk, a pinch of salt and the 50 g (2 oz) sugar. Simmer, uncovered, for 20 minutes, or until the chestnuts are tender and most of the milk has been absorbed. Strain the chestnuts and reserve the liquid.

Sieve the chestnuts into a bowl or use a food processor. Add just enough of the cooking liquid to make a purée that will hold its shape when piped. Fill a pastry bag fitted with a 2.5 mm (1/8-inch) plain tube with the purée. Pipe the purée into one large mound or individual mounds. Lightly whip the cream and flavour it with the teaspoon of sugar and the rum or brandy. Cover the top of the mound or mounds with cream. Grate the chocolate over the cream. Refrigerate until ready to serve.

If using canned purée, place it in a saucepan with the six tablespoons of cream and sugar. Whisk it over a low heat until the mixture is completely smooth. Fill the pastry bag and proceed as above.

# STRIPED SILK

20 g (¾ oz) gelatine

8 tablespoons cold water

1 litre (1¾ pints) milk

8 egg yolks

125 g (4 oz) vanilla caster sugar (page 8)

50 g (2 oz) bitter chocolate, chopped

1 teaspoon vanilla essence (not flavouring, omit if unobtainable)

40 g (1½ oz) granulated sugar

350 ml (12 fl oz) double cream, whipped lightly

**To serve:**

Bitter Chocolate Sauce (page 94)

*A spectacular striped Bavarian cream flavoured with caramel, vanilla and chocolate and served with Bitter Chocolate Sauce. The texture is beautifully silky.*

Place the gelatine with 6 tablespoons of cold water in a cup until it becomes spongy and then set the cup in hot water to dissolve the gelatine. Using a large saucepan bring the milk to the boil. Whisk the egg yolks with the vanilla caster sugar until the mixture is thick and light. Pour the hot milk over the egg yolks, whisking constantly, then return to the pan and stir with a wooden spoon over a low heat until the custard thickens enough to coat the spoon lightly. Do not allow it to boil or it will curdle. Remove the custard from the heat and stir in the gelatine.

Divide the custard between three bowls, preferably of stainless steel. Stir the chocolate into one bowl. Add the vanilla essence, if available, to the second bowl. Place the granulated sugar in a heavy-bottomed saucepan and heat until the sugar melts and caramelizes. Swirl the pan when the sugar colours and take it off the heat when it goes a rich dark brown. Add two tablespoons of water to the caramel at arms length to avoid splashes. Stir it over a low heat to blend then stir it into the third bowl.

When the custards have cooled, place the vanilla custard in iced water. When it starts to thicken fold in 125 ml (4 fl oz) of the whipped cream. Rinse a 2-litre (3½-pint) charlotte or other tall mould in cold water and shake out the excess. Spoon in the vanilla cream and refrigerate.

Set the caramel custard in iced water and when it thickens fold in 125 ml (4 fl oz) of the remaining cream. When the vanilla cream has set but is not firm carefully spoon the caramel cream over the top and refrigerate. Repeat with the chocolate cream. This may all seem very laborious but it goes very fast and there is quite a lot of flexibility

*Striped Silk* ➤

with the timing. The only danger is that if the layers set too hard the covering layer will not stick. Cover the dessert with cling film and refrigerate the terrine for at least 4 hours. It can be made up to 24 hours ahead. Unmould about 1 hour before serving. Keep it at room temperature for 20 minutes if it has been made way ahead of time as the gelatine continues to set and may become too stiff.

To serve: dip the mould in very hot water for a few seconds. Slip a knife around the edge and reverse it on to a serving plate, giving it a good shake if necessary to release the tin. Make the sauce and serve the dessert either in slices on individual plates with sauce around the edge or slice it at the table. Use a sharp hot knife when slicing and use two spatulas to help slide the slices on to the plates.

*Note:* if your mould is a metal one and worn, it may impart a metal taste to the cream. Line it with cling film or lightly oiled baking parchment.

## THREE-CHOCOLATE TERRINE

Preparation and cooking time: 55 minutes + 8 hours setting

Serves 8–12

### For the cake layer:

50 g (2 oz) butter

20 g (¾ oz) cocoa powder

1 egg

100 g (3½ oz) vanilla caster sugar (page 8)

25 g (1 oz) plain flour

### For the white layer:

1 teaspoon gelatine

6 tablespoons cold water

2 tablespoons liquid glucose or clear honey

250 g (8 oz) white chocolate, chopped into small pieces

*A three-tiered chocoholic's dream: a brownie cake layer is covered with a white chocolate mousse with a dark chocolate mousse on top of that. It is a perfect dinner party dessert because it looks as good as it tastes.*

For the cake layer: preheat the oven and line a 20 cm (8-inch) square tin with baking parchment. Melt the butter in a small saucepan over a low heat, stir in the cocoa and remove from the heat. Whisk the egg with the caster sugar and then stir in the cocoa mixture. Sift the flour over the top and fold it in. Pour the cake batter into the tin and bake it for 20 minutes. Leave it in the tin for 5 minutes, then slide a knife around the edge and turn it out on to a rack. Line a 1 kg (2 lb) loaf tin with cling film, leaving an overlap at the top to help unmould it later. Cut a piece of cake to fit the bottom of the tin and place it in the tin.

2 egg yolks

300 ml (½ pint) double cream

a pinch of salt

**For the dark layer:**

1½ teaspoons gelatine

3 tablespoons cold water

150 g (5 oz) plain chocolate

2 eggs, separated

2 tablespoons rum

75 ml (3 fl oz) whipping cream

a pinch of salt

**Oven temperature:**
Gas Mark 4/180°C/350°F

For the white chocolate layer: place the gelatine with 2 tablespoons of cold water in a small cup and leave it until it becomes spongy. Using a small heavy-bottomed saucepan bring 4 tablespoons of water and the glucose or honey to the boil. Remove the saucepan from the heat and stir in the chocolate. When the chocolate has dissolved stir in the egg yolks and salt. Set the cup with the gelatine in a pan of very hot water and leave it until it has dissolved, then pour it into the chocolate mixture. Whip the cream and fold it into the chocolate mixture, pour into the tin, and spread level. Cover the tin with cling film and refrigerate for about 1 hour or until nearly set.

For the dark chocolate layer: place the gelatine with 3 tablespoons of cold water and leave it until it becomes spongy. Melt the chocolate in the top of a double saucepan (page 10), remove it from the heat, and stir in the egg yolks and rum. Dissolve the gelatine by setting the cup in a pan of very hot water. Add the dissolved gelatine to the chocolate mixture. Whisk the egg whites with a pinch of salt until stiff and fold them into the chocolate. Lightly whip the cream and fold it into the mixture. Remove the cling film from the white chocolate. Spoon the dark chocolate mousse carefully over the white chocolate layer, spread level, cover with cling film and refrigerate until it is set, at least 8 hours.

To serve: lift the terrine out of the tin by the cling film. Cut it into thin slices using a sharp knife heated in very hot water and dried and place the slices on individual plates.

# CHOCOLATE CHESTNUT TERRINE

Preparation time: 30 minutes + 3–4 hours chilling  Serves 10–12

*150 g (5 oz) slightly salted butter, softened*

*75 g (3 oz) vanilla caster sugar (page 8)*

*250 g (8 oz) canned chestnut purée (purée de marrons)*

*175 g (6 oz) plain chocolate, chopped*

*3 tablespoons strong coffee*

*3 tablespoons rum*

*125 g (4 oz) Praline (page 87)*

**To serve:**

*Crème Anglaise (page 86)*

*A lovely chestnut dessert with a praline crust. It is served in slices with Crème Anglaise.*

Cream the butter with the sugar until light and fluffy and then stir in the chestnut purée. Melt the chocolate, coffee and rum together in the top of a double saucepan (page 10) and then beat it into the chestnut mixture. Line a 500 g (1 lb) loaf tin with cling film leaving an overlap at the top. Spoon in the mixture and spread level. Refrigerate until it is softly set, 3–4 hours. The texture is not very firm.

Spread the praline on a piece of baking parchment. Remove the chestnut terrine from the tin by pulling up the cling film. Shape the terrine into a cylinder and then remove the cling film. Roll the cylinder in the praline until all sides are well covered. Use a sharp knife dipped in hot water and dried to cut and arrange two slices on individual plates. Spoon Crème Anglaise around the edge when you are ready to serve.

*Black and White Hazelnut Terrine*

*Three-Chocolate Terrine*

*Chocolate Chestnut Terrine*

# BLACK AND WHITE HAZELNUT TERRINE

Preparation time: 50 minutes + 20 minutes baking                    Serves 12
+ chilling overnight

**For the meringue:**

*125 g (4 oz) hazelnuts*

*1 tablespoon flour*

*50 g (2 oz) vanilla caster sugar (page 8)*

*oil for greasing*

*2 egg whites*

*a pinch of salt*

**For the chocolate creams:**

*1½ teaspoons gelatine*

*6 tablespoons water*

*150 g (5 oz) white chocolate, chopped*

*1 egg yolk*

*175 g (6 oz) plain chocolate*

*75 g (3 oz) unsalted butter, cut into small pieces*

*2 tablespoons strong coffee*

*300 ml (½ pint) double cream*

*a pinch of salt*

**Oven temperature:**
*Gas Mark 4/180°C/350°F*

*Thin layers of hazelnut meringue separate a luscious black mousse from an equally luscious white one in this gourmet's dessert. It looks splendid sliced and can be served as it is or with a raspberry or chocolate sauce.*

For the meringue: preheat the oven. Lightly toast the nuts on a baking tray for 10 minutes. Keep the oven on for the meringue. Rub the nuts in a tea towel to remove most of the skins. Grind them with the flour and half of the sugar. Line an 18 × 25 cm (7 × 10-inch) shallow tin with oiled baking parchment. You can also use a larger tin and place an oiled 18 × 25 cm (7 × 10-inch) piece of baking parchment on it for easier removal. Whisk the egg whites with a pinch of salt until firm; then whisk in the remaining sugar until stiff peaks form. Fold in the nut mixture and spread over the prepared tin. Bake for 20 minutes. Leave the meringue in the tin for a few minutes before slipping a knife around the edge and inverting it on to a wire rack. Peel off the paper and leave it to cool.

For the two chocolate creams: place the gelatine with 4 tablespoons of cold water in a cup and leave it for 5 minutes until it is spongy. Place the cup in hot water and leave it until the gelatine is dissolved. Melt the white chocolate in the top of a double saucepan (page 10) then remove from the heat. Stir in the egg yolk, salt, half the dissolved gelatine and the remaining 2 table-spoons of water. Place the mixture in the refrigerator to cool. Meanwhile melt the plain chocolate (page 10). Stir in the butter and then the remaining gelatine and the coffee. Place this also in the refrigerator while you whip the cream. Fold half of the cream into the white chocolate mixture and the other half into the dark chocolate mixture. Line a hinged 8 × 25 cm (3 × 10-inch) loaf tin or an ordinary 1 kg (2 lb) loaf tin with baking parchment or cling film.

Cut the meringue into two lengths to fit the tin and place one layer in the tin. Spread the dark chocolate cream over the meringue. Set the other meringue over this and cover it with the white chocolate. Cover the tin with cling film and refrigerate overnight. Remove the terrine from the tin and slice it with a knife dipped into boiling water and dried. Centre the slices on individual plates and leave them in a cool place until ready to serve.

## CHOCOLATE AMARETTI MOUSSE

Preparation and cooking time: 20 minutes + 4 hours chilling    Serves 8

150 g (5 oz) plain chocolate, cut into small pieces

2 tablespoons rum or brandy

2 tablespoons strong coffee

1 tablespoon cocoa powder

4 eggs, separated

150 ml (5 fl oz) whipping cream

9 amaretti biscuits, crushed

a pinch of salt

*A good chocolate mousse is always appreciated and this is an exceptionally nice one. The crushed amaretti biscuits at the bottom of the mousse make the last mouthfuls a delicious surprise.*

Melt the chocolate, rum or brandy, coffee and cocoa powder in the top of a double saucepan set over simmering water. Stir until the mixture is smooth. Remove the mixture from the heat and whisk in the egg yolks, one at a time. Using a very clean bowl, preferably a copper one, whisk the egg whites with a tiny pinch of salt until they are stiff. Fold a quarter of the whites into the chocolate to lighten the mixture and then fold in the rest. Whip the cream lightly, until it holds soft peaks, and fold this into the chocolate mousse.

Place a heaped tablespoon of the crushed amaretti biscuits on a piece of cling film, seal, and set aside to decorate. Divide the rest of the biscuit crumbs between eight ramekins and then fill with the mousse. Refrigerate for 3–4 hours before serving. The mousses will keep in the refrigerator for up to two days. The mousses can also be frozen and served slightly defrosted as a parfait by leaving them 15–20 minutes at room temperature before serving. Sprinkle a little of the reserved amaretti crumbs over the mousses before serving.

# CHOCOLATE STUFFED PEARS

Preparation time: 25 minutes + 40 minutes chilling
+ 10–15 minutes cooking                                    Serves 6

**For the poached pears:**

600 ml (1 pint) water

75 g (3 oz) granulated sugar

pared rind and juice of
1 lemon

6 ripe but firm Passacrassana
or Williams pears

½ lemon

**For the mousse:**

50 g (2 oz) plain chocolate

40 g (1½ oz) butter, cut
into pieces

1 egg, separated

1 tablespoon pear liqueur
(optional)

a few grains of salt

**For the sauce:**

75 g (3 oz) caster sugar

6 tablespoons water

40 g (1½ oz) cocoa powder

25 g (1 oz) butter, cut into
pieces

*Pears and chocolate go very well together; the combination inspired the famous Pears Belle Hélène with its vanilla ice cream, poached pears and chocolate sauce. These pears are stuffed with a chocolate mousse and served cold with hot chocolate sauce.*

Using a saucepan large enough for the pears, bring the water, sugar, rind and lemon juice to a boil. Meanwhile, peel the pears but do not remove the stalks. Rub the peeled pears with the half lemon and place the pears in the saucepan. Simmer, covered, for 10–15 minutes, or until the pears are just tender. Cool the pears in the syrup for 15 minutes then drain them on a dish. When they are cold scoop out the base with a sharp spoon and remove the core.

For the mousse: first melt the chocolate (page 10). Stir in the butter and when it is blended in stir in the egg yolk and alcohol, if used. Whisk the egg white with a few grains of salt and fold it into the chocolate. Cover with cling film and refrigerate for 30–40 minutes until set.

To make the sauce: stir the first three ingredients together over a low heat until the sauce is smooth and very hot. Just before serving stir in the butter.

To serve: stuff the pears with the chocolate mousse, place them on individual plates and spoon over the hot chocolate sauce.

# SUNFLOWERS

Preparation time: 40 minutes + 2 hours chilling          Makes 8 or 12

1½ teaspoons gelatine

8 tablespoons cold water

3 eggs, separated

65 g (2½ oz) vanilla caster sugar (page 8)

200 g (7 oz) plain or bitter chocolate

65 g (2½ oz) unsalted butter, cut into small pieces

2 tablespoons rum (optional)

125 ml (4 fl oz) whipping cream, whipped

6 navel oranges

caster sugar

lemon juice

a pinch of salt

**To serve:**

cocoa powder for dusting

25 g (1 oz) Praline (page 87) or crushed amaretti biscuits

*This dessert is very pretty and tastes very very good. The flowers have chocolate centres and orange slices for petals, providing a lovely contrast of tastes and colours.*

Place the gelatine with 2 tablespoons of cold water in a cup and leave it until it becomes spongy, then set the cup in hot water to dissolve the gelatine. Whisk the egg yolks, remaining water and 50 g (2 oz) of the sugar in a heatproof bowl set over simmering water, until the mixture is thick and foamy. Remove it from the heat, add the gelatine, and continue to whisk for a few more minutes.

Melt the chocolate in the top of a double saucepan (page 10). Whisk in the butter, a little at a time. If the mixture is too stiff, place it over a medium heat and whisk it until the consistency lightens and will blend more easily with the egg mixture. Then stir in the rum if you are using it. Carefully fold the chocolate into the egg mixture. Whisk the egg whites with a good pinch of salt until just stiff, then whisk in the remaining sugar, beating until glossy, and fold into the chocolate mixture. Carefully fold in the whipped cream. Line eight 100 ml (3½ fl oz) or twelve 6 cm (2½-inch) ramekins with cling film. Spoon in the chocolate mousse, cover with cling film and refrigerate for at least 2 hours.

With a serrated knife, peel the oranges as you would an apple, removing all traces of pith and skin. Cut the orange segments away from the membrane, working over a bowl to catch the juices. Sprinkle the orange segments with caster sugar and lemon juice, then cover them with cling film and refrigerate.

To serve: turn out the chocolate mousses on to a piece of baking parchment. Sift cocoa powder over the tops and sprinkle with a little Praline or biscuit crumbs. Use a spatula to lift each mousse to the centre of individual serving plates. Place orange segments around the mousse to form petals.

*Variation:* sift cocoa powder over the top of the mousses in the same way as for Sunflowers. Spoon some Pistachio Sauce (page 92) or Crème Anglaise (page 86) on to each serving plate and set the chocolate mousse in the centre. Cover the top of the mousse with flecks of silver paper called warq. This is an edible paper obtainable from Indian grocers.

# PETITS POTS AU MOCHA ET CHOCOLAT

Preparation time for mocha petits pots: 10 minutes          Serves 4
+ 30 minutes cooking + 30 minutes chilling
Preparation time for chocolate petits pots: 10 minutes + 3 hours chilling

**For the mocha petits pots:**

*300 ml (½ pint) single cream*

*2 tablespoons medium-ground coffee*

*50 g (2 oz) plain chocolate, chopped*

*1 tablespoon caster sugar*

*4 egg yolks*

**For the chocolate petits pots:**

*300 ml (½ pint) double cream*

*175 g (6 oz) plain or bitter chocolate, chopped*

*1 tablespoon orange liqueur or liqueur of your choice*

*a tiny pinch of salt*

**Oven temperature:**
*Gas Mark 2/150°C/300°F*

*Both these little custards have a smooth creamy texture and an excellent flavour. The chocolate version does not have to be baked because the chocolate 'seizes' when it is stirred into the boiling cream, which thickens it.*

For the mocha petits pots: preheat the oven. Bring the cream and ground coffee slowly to the boil. Remove from the heat, stir a few times and strain through a very fine sieve or a coffee filter paper. Whisk in the chocolate and the sugar and when it is smooth whisk in the egg yolks, one at a time. Taste and add more sugar if wished. Divide the mixture between four ramekins and place them in a bain marie or roasting tin. Pour in enough hot water to come two-thirds up the sides of the ramekins, cover with foil and place in the oven for about 20 minutes or until just set. Chill for 30 minutes and serve with biscuits such as Florentines (page 78).

For the chocolate petits pots: bring the cream to a good boil, remove from the heat and whisk in the chopped chocolate. When the mixture is smooth, stir in the liqueur and salt. Divide between four ramekins or mousse pots and place them in the refrigerator for at least 3 hours to set.

# MARQUISE AU CHOCOLAT BLANC

Preparation time: 45 minutes + 35 minutes cooking
+ 24 hours chilling

Serves 10

**For the cake layer:**

75 g (3 oz) plain flour, plus
extra for dusting

3 eggs

75 g (3 oz) vanilla caster
sugar (page 8)

40 g (1½ oz) butter,
melted, plus extra for
greasing

a pinch of salt

**For the mousse:**

1 teaspoon gelatine

7 tablespoons cold water

2 level tablespoons liquid
glucose or clear honey

300 g (10 oz) white
chocolate, chopped into
small pieces

3 egg yolks

350 ml (12 fl oz) double
cream

a pinch of salt

**For the chocolate sauce:**

100 g (3½ oz) vanilla
caster sugar

150 ml (5 fl oz) water

50 g (2 oz) cocoa powder

**Oven temperature:**
Gas Mark 4/180°C/350°F

*Mont Diavolo* ➤
*Marquise au Chocolat Blanc*

*A delectable dessert inspired by nouvelle cuisine, this
is a terrine of white chocolate mousse and sponge cake
served in slices on a bed of dark chocolate sauce.*

Preheat the oven. For the cake: butter and flour a
20 cm (8-inch) cake tin and line the bottom with
baking parchment. Sift the flour with the salt
three times. Break the eggs into a large bowl,
preferably a copper one, and set it over a pan of
very hot water. Add the sugar and whisk the
mixture for about 8 minutes using an electric
hand-held beater or wire whisk, until it has
doubled in volume and leaves a ribbon trail
when the whisk is lifted. Sift the flour over the
mixture a third at a time, folding in each batch
carefully with a large metal spoon; then fold in
the melted butter. Turn the mixture into the
prepared tin and bake for 35 minutes. Leave it in
the tin for a few minutes before turning it out on
to a rack to cool.

For the mousse: place the gelatine with 2 tablespoons of cold water in a cup and leave it for
5 minutes until it is spongy. Then place the cup
in very hot water and leave until the gelatine is
dissolved. Bring 5 tablespoons of water with the
glucose or honey to the boil, remove from the
heat and stir in the white chocolate, salt and
gelatine. When the mixture is smooth stir in the
egg yolks. Lightly whip the cream and carefully
fold it into the chocolate mixture. Spoon the
mixture into a 500 g (1 lb) ungreased loaf tin and
cover with the sponge, cut to fit. Place it in the
refrigerator and leave for 24 hours.

For the sauce: simply dissolve the sugar in the
water, bring to the boil and whisk in the cocoa.

To serve: place the tin in very hot water for a
few seconds and then turn it out. Slice with a
sharp knife heated in hot water and dried. Place a
slice on individual serving plates and surround it
with some chocolate sauce.

# MONT DIAVOLO

Preparation and cooking time: 1¼ hours + 8 hours chilling     Serves 12

**For the cake:**

100 g (3½ oz) plain flour

40 g (1½ oz) cocoa powder

½ teaspoon baking powder

4 eggs

150 g (5 oz) vanilla caster sugar (page 8), plus extra for dusting

40 g (1½ oz) unsalted butter

a pinch of salt

**For the filling:**

25 g (1 oz) gelatine

4 tablespoons water

6 eggs, separated

50 g (2 oz) vanilla caster sugar

900 ml (1½ pints) whipping cream

325 g (11 oz) plain chocolate, chopped very finely

a pinch of salt

300 ml (½ pint) double cream

**For the icing:**

150 g (5 oz) plain chocolate, chopped

40 g (1½ oz) unsalted butter, plus extra for greasing

2 tablespoons milk

**Oven temperature:**
Gas Mark 4/180°C/350°F

*This is a spectacular dessert, the kind that your guests will go home talking about. A mountain of chocolate mousse is hidden under a layer of sponge cake covered in chocolate icing.*

For the cake: preheat the oven. Line a 30 × 36 cm (12 × 14-inch) baking tray with baking parchment. Sift the flour, cocoa, baking powder and salt together three times. Break the eggs into a large heatproof bowl, preferably a copper one, and set it over a pan of very hot but not boiling water. Using an electric hand-held beater, whisk the eggs with the vanilla caster sugar for 6–8 minutes, until the mixture has doubled in volume and is thick enough to leave a ribbon trail when the whisk is lifted. Melt the butter over a gentle heat. Sift the dry ingredients over the egg mixture a third at a time, folding in each batch carefully with a large metal spoon, and then fold in the melted butter. Pour the mixture into the prepared tin and bake for 12 minutes or until springy to the touch. Cool for a few minutes before cutting around the edge and reversing it on to a lightly sugared piece of baking parchment. Peel away the baking parchment and set the cake aside.

For the filling: place the gelatine with the water in a small cup and leave it until it is spongy. Whisk the egg yolks with the sugar until they are light and thick. Bring the whipping cream to the boil and pour it over the egg yolks, whisking continuously. Pour the mixture back into the saucepan and stir it constantly with a wooden spoon over a very low heat until the mixture thickens and coats the back of the spoon. Take care not to let the mixture come near to boiling point or it will curdle. Remove from the heat and stir in the chocolate until it is well blended. Place the cup with the gelatine in a small saucepan of very hot water and leave it until the gelatine is dissolved;

then stir it into the chocolate cream. Cool the chocolate cream by placing it in the refrigerator or setting the bowl in iced water. Whisk the egg whites with a pinch of salt, carefully fold in the double cream; then fold into the chocolate cream.

Lightly butter and sugar a 2.75–3 litre (5½–6-pint) pudding basin and line the base with a round of baking parchment. Then line the basin with cake, first cutting out a round to fit the bottom and then strips for the sides. Pour the chocolate cream into the basin, cover it with cling film and refrigerate until set, at least 8 hours.

For the icing: place all the icing ingredients in the top of a double saucepan set over simmering water and stir until smooth. Trim the cake to make the dessert have an even base. Slip a knife around the inside edge of the basin and turn the dessert out on to a large serving plate. Cover the cake with the icing using a spatula or palette knife. Keep refrigerated until ready to serve.

To serve: cut it into wedges with a sharp knife dipped in hot water and dried.

# EASY CHOCOLATE GINGER PUDDING

Preparation time: 15 minutes + 30 minutes freezing or 1½ hours chilling                    Serves 6–8

oil for greasing

100 g (3½ oz) plain chocolate, chopped

65 g (2½ oz) butter

1 egg, separated

25 g (1 oz) icing sugar, sifted, plus extra for dusting

75 g (3 oz) ginger snaps, chopped into small pieces

40 g (1½ oz) stem ginger, chopped

2 teaspoons syrup from the jar of stem ginger

*This combines two of my husband's favourite foods, chocolate and ginger snaps. It is a handy recipe because you can concoct it in minutes and pop it in the freezer, where it will quickly set.*

Oil an 18 cm (7-inch) flan tin with a removable base. Using a heavy-bottomed saucepan melt the chocolate and butter together over a very gentle heat, stirring continuously. When the mixture is smooth remove it from the heat and whisk in the egg yolk. Whisk the egg white until it is stiff, add the sugar and continue to whisk until it becomes glossy and very stiff. Pour the chocolate mixture over it and fold in using a large metal spoon. Fold in the ginger snaps, stem ginger and syrup.

Pour the batter into the prepared tin and smooth it level with a spatula. Cover with cling film or foil and either freeze it for about 30 minutes or refrigerate it for 1½ hours or until set. Remove it from the tin, dust with icing sugar and serve in small wedges with a dollop of whipped cream.

# PRUNE NUT CHOCOLATE FOOL

Preparation time: 40 minutes + 4 hours chilling                    Serves 8

2 tablespoons Armagnac or Cognac

250 g (8 oz) cooked pitted prunes, chopped

1 tablespoon gelatine

2 tablespoons cold water

325 ml (11 fl oz) milk

¼ teaspoon cinnamon

3 eggs, separated

100 g (3½ oz) vanilla caster sugar (page 8)

125 g (4 oz) plain chocolate, chopped

125 ml (4 fl oz) whipping cream, whipped

50 g (2 oz) walnuts, chopped

a pinch of salt

**To decorate:**

white chocolate curls (page 12)

*Prunes and nuts go well with chocolate and together they make an unusual and delicious dessert.*

Mix the Armagnac or Cognac with the prunes, cover and leave overnight if possible or for as long as is available. Place the gelatine with the water in a cup and leave it until it becomes spongy, then set the cup in hot water to dissolve the gelatine. Bring the milk and cinnamon to the boil in a heavy saucepan. Whisk the egg yolks with half the sugar in a bowl. Pour the hot milk over the egg yolks, whisking continuously, then return the mixture to the saucepan and stir until the custard thickens slightly. Do not allow it to boil or it will curdle. Remove the custard from the heat and stir in the chocolate, and when it is blended add the gelatine.

Set the bowl in iced water and stir occasionally until it starts to thicken. Fold in the cream, prunes and nuts. Whisk the egg whites with a pinch of salt until they are stiff, add the remaining sugar and whisk for a few seconds more. Fold the egg whites into the chocolate mixture. Divide the dessert between eight ramekins or wine glasses and refrigerate them for at least 4 hours.

They will keep for up to three days if covered and refrigerated. Leave them at room temperature for about 1 hour before serving. Sprinkle a few white chocolate curls over the tops.

# COLD ZABAGLIONE WITH CHOCOLATE

Preparation time: 10 minutes + 30 minutes chilling     Serves 4–6

1 teaspoon gelatine

1 tablespoon cold water

4 egg yolks

3 tablespoons caster sugar

125 ml (4 fl oz) Marsala

75 ml (3 fl oz) whipping cream

**To serve:**

40 g (1½ oz) plain chocolate, refrigerated

*This is simply gorgeous, a foamy zabaglione with a thin layer of grated chocolate. The chocolate and zabaglione melt in the mouth but not before you have savoured their different and complementary flavours.*

Place the gelatine with the cold water in a cup and leave it for 5 minutes until it is spongy. Place the cup in a pan of very hot water and leave the gelatine to dissolve.

Place the egg yolks, sugar and Marsala in a bowl, preferably a copper one, and set it over a pan of barely simmering water. Whisk until the mixture is thick enough to leave a ribbon trail when the whisk is lifted. Be careful not to allow the mixture to become too hot or it will curdle. Remove it from the heat, whisk in the gelatine, and continue to whisk for 2–3 minutes until the mixture cools. Whip the cream and gently fold it into the egg mixture. Fill goblets.or ramekins with the zabaglione and refrigerate for 30 minutes.

Using a sharp knife make very fine shavings of chocolate. Sprinkle a fine covering of the chocolate over the top of the zabaglione immediately before serving.

*Note:* this dessert can also be served at once at room temperature.

# TIRAMI SU

125 ml (4 fl oz) brandy

125 ml (4 fl oz) Marsala

250 ml (8 fl oz) strong
expresso coffee or very
strong coffee

32 sponge fingers

3 eggs, separated

3 tablespoons vanilla caster
sugar (page 8)

325 g (11 oz) mascarpone
cheese or ½ quantity cream
cheese and ½ double cream

65 g (2½ oz) plain
chocolate, refrigerated

a pinch of salt

*A luxurious Italian-style trifle very popular in Italy
today. Its name 'pick me up' derives, understandably,
from the ingredients.*

Mix the brandy and Marsala together then add
half of this to the coffee. Place 16 sponge fingers
in the bottom of a 1.5–1.75-litre (2½–3-pint)
gratin or other shallow dish and sprinkle with
half of the coffee mixture. Whisk the egg yolks
with the sugar until thick and pale and then
blend in the mascarpone or cream cheese and
double cream and stir in the remaining brandy
mixture.

Whisk the egg whites with a pinch of salt until
stiff peaks form and fold them into the cheese
mixture. Spoon half of this mixture over the
sponge fingers. Dip the remaining sponge
fingers into the rest of the coffee mixture and
place them on top of the cream in the dish.
Spread the rest of the cream over this. Grate the
chocolate on the coarse side of a grater or in a
rotary hand grinder. Sprinkle the chocolate over
the top of the cream. Cover and refrigerate for at
least 8 hours.

# FROZEN DESSERTS, ICE CREAMS AND SORBETS

## ICED CHOCOLATE SOUFFLÉS

Preparation time: 45 minutes + 3 hours freezing                    Serves 4
+ 1½ hours to soften

*25 g (1 oz) cocoa powder*

*50 g (2 oz) plain chocolate, chopped*

*125 ml (4 fl oz) water*

*100 g (3½ oz) vanilla caster sugar (page 8)*

*2 egg whites*

*2 tablespoons Grand Marnier or white rum*

*300 ml (½ pint) double cream, whipped*

**To decorate:**

*chocolate curls (page 12)*

*You don't have to worry about these soufflés puffing up since paper collars give them their raised appearance. The mixture will also set to a perfect airy consistency without any stirring in the freezer.*

Prepare individual ramekins by wrapping a collar of baking parchment around each one to extend 3.5 cm (1½ inches) above the top of the dish and tape in place. Melt the cocoa, chocolate and 4 tablespoons of the water together in the top of a double saucepan set over hot but not boiling water. In a heavy-bottomed small saucepan dissolve the sugar in the remaining water, bring it to the boil and boil without stirring until the temperature reaches 115°C/ 239°F on a sugar thermometer (soft ball stage – when a drop of the mixture in cold water forms a soft ball). While the sugar is boiling, whisk the egg whites until stiff. Pour the hot sugar syrup in a steady stream over the whites, while continuing to whisk, and keep whisking until the mixture is thick and cool, about 10 minutes. Use a large metal spoon to fold the chocolate into the whites, and then fold in the alcohol and the whipped cream. Spoon into the ramekins and freeze for at least 3 hours until firm. They can be frozen for two weeks if completely wrapped. Before serving, remove the ramekins from the freezer and leave them in the refrigerator for about 1½ hours to soften. Peel away the paper collars and decorate with Chocolate Curls.

# CHOCOLATE COATED ICE CREAM BALLS

Preparation and cooking time: 30 minutes          Serves 6–8
+ 4 hours freezing

*Vanilla Ice Cream (page 39)
or Old-Fashioned Chocolate
Ice Cream (page 43) or
½ quantity of both*

*250 g (8 oz) plain cooking
chocolate*

*A pyramid of smooth chocolate balls on a pretty
serving plate will charm your guests even before they
have had a taste.*

Make the ice cream and freeze. Line a baking
tray that will fit in your freezer with baking
parchment. Make round balls from the ice cream
using an ice cream scoop and place them on the
paper. Place the tray back in the freezer until the
balls are very hard, 2–3 hours. Melt half the
chocolate in the top of a double saucepan
(page 10) and cool. Use a spoon to help roll half
the balls, one at a time, in the chocolate. The
cold ice cream sets the chocolate almost instantly.
Place the balls back on the tray and work as
quickly as possible. It may be necessary to place
the chocolate back over the hot water to reheat it
slightly if it starts to harden. Place the tray back
in the freezer. Repeat with the remaining
chocolate and ice cream balls. Serve the balls the
same day.

*Chocolate Coated
Ice Cream Balls*

*Ice Cream Bombe*

*Iced Chocolate Soufflé*

37

# ICE CREAM BOMBE

Preparation time: 50 minutes + 8 hours freezing          Serves 12

*Vanilla Ice Cream (page 39)*

*Chocolate Amaretti Mousse (page 23) omitting the amaretti biscuits*

*Ice cream bombes are among the most satisfying and festive of desserts and their possibilities are endless. An outer ice cream layer, or two different ones, cover a softer mousse centre. In this bombe, vanilla ice cream hides a chocolate mousse. It may seem a conventional combination but it is a great one, and with the current rage for innovation is sometimes overlooked. For a more unusual bombe try two layers of ice cream, white and dark chocolate, with a Kumquat Sorbet (page 40) centre.*

Prepare the vanilla ice cream. Leave the ice cream at room temperature for 35–45 minutes to soften slightly. Chill a 1.5-litre (2½-pint) bombe mould or pudding basin in the freezer.

Meanwhile make the chocolate mousse following the recipe on page 23, leaving out the biscuits.

Line the mould with the vanilla ice cream by spooning it in from the bottom upwards, and pressing it into a smooth even layer about 1 cm (½-inch) thick. Pour the mousse in the centre, cover it with cling film and freeze for 4 hours. Use the bombe within a week.

To serve: dip the mould for 5 seconds in a bowl of cold water (cold water prevents the ice cream from melting too much), uncover and reverse on to a serving dish giving a sharp shake to release the mould.

# VANILLA ICE CREAM

Preparation and cooking time: 30 minutes      Makes 1 litre (1¾ pints)
+ 4 hours freezing

*600 ml (1 pint) milk*

*1 vanilla pod, split lengthways*

*5 egg yolks*

*125 g (4 oz) vanilla caster sugar (page 8)*

*300 ml (½ pint) double cream*

*1 teaspoon vanilla essence (not flavouring, omit if unavailable)*

*Vanilla ice cream was made for chocolate, which heightens its flavour and provides a soothing contrast. A home-made vanilla ice cream with a good chocolate sauce is unbeatable. See page 94 for a variety of chocolate sauces.*

Bring the milk and vanilla pod to just below boiling point, cover and leave to infuse for 15 minutes. Scrape some of the black seeds from the pod into the milk. Wash and dry the pod and store with caster sugar to make vanilla sugar. Whisk the egg yolks and sugar together until pale and thick. Whisk in the milk, and then return the mixture to the saucepan. Place over a very low heat, stirring constantly with a wooden spoon, until the custard thickens slightly. Your finger should leave a clear trail when drawn across the back of the spoon. Do not allow the custard to come near the boil or it will curdle. Strain the custard into a bowl and allow to cool. Whip the cream to just soft peak stage and fold it into the cool custard. Taste and add the vanilla essence if available. Pour the mixture into an ice cream maker or a metal container. Follow the directions given with your ice cream maker. Otherwise set the container in the freezing compartment of the refrigerator or the fast-freeze section of the freezer and freeze until it is frozen, about 3 hours. Remove it from the freezer, chop it into several chunks and put it into a chilled processor or blender and process it until smooth. Return it to freeze for at least another hour before serving.

# KUMQUAT SORBET IN A CHOCOLATE BOX

Preparation time: 2 hours + 6 hours freezing                    Serves 8

**For the sorbet:**

10 sugar cubes

18 blood oranges or 10 large oranges, to make 750 ml (1¼ pints) of juice

150 g (5 oz) kumquats

150 g (5 oz) granulated sugar, plus extra

125 ml (4 fl oz) water

juice of 1 lemon

**For the chocolate boxes:**

32 × 5 cm (2-inch) square, thin pieces of chocolate (page 12) made from 375 g (12 oz) plain chocolate

8 × 5 cm (2-inch) square, thin pieces of sponge cake

apricot jam

*Use blood oranges when they are in season and you will have a beautiful red sorbet flecked with orange kumquats. Serve it piled high in a chocolate box or cup and I promise it will become one of your favourite desserts.*

Rub the sugar cubes all over the orange skins until they become pale yellow. Wash and cut the kumquats in quarters, lengthways. Remove any pips. Place them in a small saucepan with the sugar cubes, granulated sugar and water. Simmer very gently for about 25 minutes, until the kumquats are tender. Remove the saucepan from the heat and set aside.

Meanwhile squeeze the oranges and strain the juice. You will need 750 ml (1¼ pints) of strained juice. Strain the kumquat syrup into the orange juice. Add half of the lemon juice and taste. You are after a sharp yet sweet taste. The flavour will lessen once it freezes. Adjust the flavour by adding more lemon juice or sugar. Chop the kumquats into tiny pieces and add them to the syrup. Pour the mixture into an ice cream maker or metal container. Follow the directions given with your ice cream maker. Otherwise set the container in the fast-freeze section of the freezer or the freezer compartment of the refrigerator for about 3 hours. Chop the sorbet into several chunks, put them into a chilled processor and process until smooth. Return the sorbet to the freezer for at least another 3 hours.

To make the chocolate boxes: make the chocolate squares following the directions on page 12 for cut-out shapes. For each box, coat the sides of one square of sponge with apricot jam and attach the chocolate sides to it. Carefully fill the chocolate boxes with the sorbet and set in

*Kumquat Sorbet in a Chocolate Box*

the freezer until ready to serve. Use the dessert the same day as you assemble it.

The sorbet also looks attractive served in scoops with a chocolate leaf or two on the top or served in chocolate cups or baskets (page 11–12).

## CHOCOLATE SORBET

Preparation time: 40 minutes + 4 hours freezing

Makes 1 litre (1¾ pints)

1 teaspoon gelatine

600 ml (1 pint) cold water, plus 2 tablespoons

175 g (6 oz) vanilla caster sugar (page 8)

150 ml (5 fl oz) single cream

2 egg yolks

175 g (6 oz) bitter chocolate, chopped

*If you are looking for something chocolaty but not too rich, this sorbet is the perfect solution. It can be served on its own or with a sauce such as Pistachio Sauce (page 92).*

Place the gelatine with 2 tablespoons of cold water and leave it until it becomes spongy. Heat the sugar with 600 ml (1 pint) of water until the sugar has dissolved then bring the mixture to the boil and boil for 5 minutes. Set it aside to cool down.

Then place the cream, egg yolks and chocolate in the top of a double saucepan set over barely simmering water and stir until smooth. Remove the mixture from the heat. Set the cup with the gelatine in very hot water and leave it until the gelatine has completely dissolved; then stir it into the sugar syrup. Add the sugar syrup to the chocolate cream. Pour the mixture into an ice cream maker or a metal container. Follow the directions given with your ice cream maker. Otherwise set the container in the freezing compartment of the refrigerator or the fast-freeze section of the freezer and freeze until it is frozen, about 3 hours. Remove it from the freezer, chop it into several chunks and put it into a chilled processor or blender and process it until smooth. Return to freeze for at least another hour before serving.

# OLD-FASHIONED CHOCOLATE ICE CREAM

Preparation and cooking time:
30 minutes + 3 hours freezing

Makes about 1 litre (1¾ pints)

*175 g (6 oz) plain chocolate*

*450 ml (¾ pint) milk*

*5 egg yolks*

*125 g (4 oz) vanilla caster sugar (page 8)*

*300 ml (½ pint) double cream, whipped lightly*

*This is a lovely creamy ice cream, smooth and chocolaty without being overwhelmingly rich. For an extra treat you can turn it into Praline Ice Cream (see below).*

Melt the chocolate in the top of a double saucepan (page 10) and set aside. Bring the milk to just below boiling point. Whisk the egg yolks with the sugar in a bowl until thick and light and then whisk in the hot milk. Return the mixture to the saucepan and stir continually with a wooden spoon over a very gentle heat until the custard thickens just enough to coat the spoon and leave a trail when your finger is drawn across the back of the spoon. Do not allow it to boil or it will curdle. Stir in the melted chocolate and strain into a bowl. Refrigerate until cool and then fold in the lightly whipped cream. Turn the mixture into an ice cream maker or a metal container. Follow the maker's instructions, otherwise set in the freezing compartment of a refrigerator or place in the fast-freeze section of a freezer until set, about 3 hours.

To serve: remove the ice cream from the freezer about 10 minutes before serving to allow it to soften slightly.

*Chocolate Praline Ice Cream:* when the ice cream has partially set, stir in 100 g (3½ oz) of Praline (page 87). If the ice cream has frozen solid, cut it into a few chunks, place in a processor, and whizz it up for a minute to soften before adding the praline.

# WHITE CHOCOLATE ICE CREAM

Preparation time: 30 minutes
+ 3 hours freezing

Makes 900 ml (1½ pints)

150 g (5 oz) white
chocolate, chopped

300 ml (½ pint) milk

75 g (3 oz) vanilla caster
sugar (page 8)

400 ml (14 fl oz) double
cream

*This ice cream has the flavour of white chocolate and is
particularly good served simply in a chocolate shell
(page 12) or combined with a dark chocolate sauce or
fruit. See suggestions below.*

Place the white chocolate with 4 tablespoons of
the milk in the top of a double saucepan set over
hot but not boiling water. Cover and leave it to
melt. Meanwhile dissolve the sugar in the
remaining milk on a gentle heat. Allow the milk
to cool to room temperature before stirring in
the melted chocolate. Whip the cream to the soft
peak stage and fold it into the chocolate mixture.
Freeze in an ice cream maker or in the fast-freeze
section of a freezer until firm, approximately
3 hours.

*Cherries Jubilee:* heat 175 g (6 oz) morello
cherries with 2 tablespoons of their syrup. Heat
5 tablespoons of kirsch, Cognac or Armagnac in
another small pan, and then ignite it and pour
over the hot cherries. Serve with the white
chocolate ice cream.

*White Chocolate Ice Cream with Marmalade
Sauce:* make the sauce (page 92) and pour it over
scoops of the ice cream while still warm.

*White Chocolate Ice Cream with Bitter Chocolate
Sauce:* make the sauce (page 92) and serve it hot
or cold with the ice cream.

*White Chocolate Ice Cream with Kumquats:*
make the poached kumquats (page 48) and serve
with the ice cream.

*White Chocolate Ice Cream in a chocolate shell*
*Chocolate Semifreddo*

# CHOCOLATE SEMIFREDDO

Preparation time: 10 minutes + 8 hours freezing    Serves 8

*350 ml (12 fl oz) double cream*

*125 g (4 oz) icing sugar, sifted*

*4 egg whites*

*75 g (3 oz) plain chocolate, grated (page 12)*

*3 tablespoons curaçao or other orange liqueur or rum*

*A lovely simple frozen dessert with a light, melting consistency. It can be whisked up in a matter of minutes and popped into the freezer, ready to grace any occasion.*

Line a 1 kg (2 lb) loaf tin with cling film allowing a good overlap. Whip the cream with half the sugar until it holds soft peaks. Whisk the egg whites until stiff; then whisk in the remaining sugar and whisk a few seconds more until they are thick and glossy. Fold the whites into the cream and then fold in the chocolate and the liqueur or rum. Spoon the mixture into the tin and spread level. Cover it with another piece of cling film and freeze for at least 8 hours or overnight.

To serve: lift the Semifreddo out of the tin using the cling film. Remove the cling film, cut the Semifreddo into slices and place them on individual plates.

# HOT DESSERTS

## NEW-STYLE CHOCOLATE SOUFFLÉ

Preparation time: 30 minutes + 10 or 25 minutes baking          Serves 6

butter for greasing

175 g (6 oz) plain chocolate, chopped

250 ml (8 fl oz) double cream

5 egg yolks

3 tablespoons rum or strong coffee

7 egg whites

a pinch of cream of tartar

4 tablespoons caster sugar, plus extra for dusting

a pinch of salt

**To serve:**

Crème Anglaise (page 86) or 300 ml (½ pint) whipping cream, whipped

**Oven temperature:**
Gas Mark 7/220°C/425°F

*This is a gorgeous flour-less soufflé popular with nouvelle cuisine chefs. It looks particularly nice served in individual soufflé dishes.*

Preheat the oven. Butter and sugar six 300 ml (½-pint) soufflé ramekins or a 1.75-litre (3-pint) soufflé dish. Using a heavy-bottomed saucepan, stir the chocolate and double cream together over a low heat until well blended. Remove from the heat and immediately whisk in the egg yolks, one at a time, and then the rum or coffee.

Whisk the egg whites with a pinch of salt and cream of tartar in a very clean bowl, preferably a copper one, until the mixture reaches the soft peak stage. Sprinkle the sugar over the top and continue to whisk until the egg whites are glossy and stiff.

Gently heat the chocolate mixture, stirring, until hand hot. Fold in a large spoonful of the whites to lighten the chocolate mixture before pouring it over the whites and carefully folding all together. Fill the prepared dishes to within 1 cm (½ inch) of the rim. Run the point of a knife around the edge of the soufflés to make them rise in a 'top hat' shape. Place on a baking sheet and bake the small soufflés for 10 minutes or a large one for 25 minutes. Serve immediately and pass the Crème Anglaise or lightly whipped cream separately.

# CHOCOLATE KUMQUAT CAKE

Preparation time: 35 minutes + 30 minutes baking          Serves 8–10

**For the poached kumquats:**

500 g (1 lb) kumquats

150 g (5 oz) granulated sugar

300 ml (½ pint) water

**For the cake:**

45 g (1¾ oz) self-raising flour

150 g (5 oz) vanilla caster sugar (page 8)

3 large eggs (size 2)

75 g (3 oz) bitter chocolate, broken into pieces

25 g (1 oz) cocoa powder

125 g (4 oz) unsalted butter, plus extra for greasing

a pinch of salt

**For the glaze:**

125 g (4 oz) plain chocolate

25 g (1 oz) unsalted butter

2 tablespoons milk

**Oven temperature:**
Gas Mark 2/150°C/300°F

*A flat, rich cake glazed with chocolate and served still warm with poached kumquats in a tangy syrup.*

Preheat the oven. For the poached kumquats: wash the kumquats, remove the stalks and halve them lengthways. Place them in a pan with the sugar and water. Bring to the boil and simmer very gently for 30 minutes. Serve the warm poached kumquats with slices of the cake.

For the cake: grease a 20 cm (8-inch) shallow, round cake tin and line the bottom with baking parchment. Set a large heatproof bowl over hot water and beat the flour, salt, sugar and eggs together with an electric beater or wire whisk for about 10 minutes. The mixture should become very thick and leave a ribbon trail when the whisk is lifted. Meanwhile, melt the chocolate, cocoa and butter together in the top of a double saucepan (page 10). Add this to the egg mixture and continue to whisk for another 8 minutes. Pour the mixture into the prepared tin and bake in the oven for 25–30 minutes until the cake is springy to the touch. When the cake is ready, remove it from the oven and leave in the tin for 10 minutes. Turn it out on to a cake rack, remove the baking parchment and glaze the cake.

Make the glaze while the cake is baking. Melt all the ingredients in a double saucepan set over barely simmering water until smooth. Let the glaze cool slightly so it will thicken a little. Set a plate under the cake rack to catch excess glaze. Pour the glaze over the cake while both are still warm and spread evenly with a palette knife. Leave the glazed cake for 10 minutes to set before serving. Decorate the cake with some of the poached kumquats.

*Chocolate Kumquat Cake*

# CHOCOLATE AMARETTI FILLED CRÊPES

Preparation time: 45 minutes + 30 minutes resting           Serves 4–6

### For the crêpes:

125 g (4 oz) plain flour

250 ml (8 fl oz) milk

3 eggs

2 tablespoons unsalted butter, melted

oil for greasing

a pinch of salt

### For the filling:

275 ml (9 fl oz) milk

3 egg yolks

65 g (2½ oz) vanilla caster sugar (page 8)

25 g (1 oz) plain flour

65 g (2½ oz) plain chocolate, chopped

1 tablespoon almond liqueur such as Amaretto di Saronno

150 ml (5 fl oz) whipping cream, whipped

50 g (2 oz) amaretti biscuits, crushed, or Praline (page 87)

melted butter and sugar, plus extra butter for greasing

3–4 tablespoons of brandy or cognac for flaming (optional)

### Oven temperature:
Gas Mark 4 / 180°C / 350°F

*Paper-thin crêpes rolled around a luscious chocolate cream are a grand way to end a special meal. They can be prepared ahead of time and simply heated and flamed at the last moment.*

For the crêpes: first sift the flour and salt into a bowl. Make a well in the centre and add the milk and eggs. Whisk from the centre, slowly blending the ingredients, then add the melted butter. Be careful not to overmix. Leave the batter to rest for at least 30 minutes. It should have the consistency of thin cream. Add a few tablespoons of water if necessary.

Brush the inside of a crêpe or frying pan 23 cm (9 inches) in diameter with oil. Heat the pan until quite hot, add a serving spoon of batter to the pan and then tilt it to coat the bottom evenly. Pour out any excess batter and the next time use less. Cook over a high heat until it is browned, then turn the crêpe over and cook for 10 seconds on the second side. It may take a few crêpes before the consistency, amount of batter and heat are just right. Pile them on a plate. They can be kept refrigerated for two days, or frozen if a layer of cling film or baking parchment is placed between each crêpe.

For the filling: bring the milk to the boil. Whisk the egg yolks, sugar and flour together in a bowl. Whisk in the hot milk and then return the mixture to the saucepan and simmer for 2–3 minutes, stirring constantly. Remove from the heat and stir in the chocolate and the tablespoon of liqueur. When the chocolate cream is cool, fold in the lightly whipped cream and the amaretti crumbs or Praline.

Preheat the oven. Grease a large flameproof gratin dish with butter. Place a spoonful of the filling on the underside of a crêpe, roll it up and place it seam-side down in the dish; or fold the crêpes into quarters and overlap them in the dish. Continue until all the crêpes are used.

Brush the tops with melted butter and a sprinkling of sugar. Cover them with a piece of baking parchment. Bake for 15–20 minutes or until hot. If using it, heat the liqueur in a small pan, flame it and pour it over the crêpes. Serve immediately.

The filling can be made up to two days ahead if refrigerated but fill the crêpes the same day as you serve them.

# BITTER CHOCOLATE SOUFFLÉ

Preparation time: 20 minutes + 35 minutes baking                    Serves 4

100 g (3½ oz) bitter chocolate

3 tablespoons cornflour

250 ml (8 fl oz) milk

50 g (2 oz) vanilla caster sugar (page 8), plus extra for dusting

3 tablespoons Grand Marnier, Cointreau or curaçao

a knob of butter, plus extra for greasing

5 egg whites

3 egg yolks

a pinch of salt

**To serve:**

Crème Anglaise (page 86) or 175 ml (6 fl oz) whipped cream

**Oven temperature:**
Gas Mark 5/190°C/375°F

*What could be nicer than a beautiful, light-as-air chocolate soufflé? It is not difficult to make and can sit quite happily for a few hours, even with the whites folded in, before being baked. The only danger is overcooking, which makes it dry and tough.*

Preheat the oven. Butter and sugar a 1-litre (1¾-pint) soufflé dish. Make a collar with a folded strip of baking parchment 10 cm (4 inches) wide and long enough to go around the dish with a good overlap. Butter and sugar the inside of the strip and tie it securely to the dish.

Melt the chocolate (page 10) and set it aside. Mix the cornflour to a smooth paste with a few tablespoons of the milk and then gradually stir in the rest of the milk. Pour it into a saucepan and bring to the boil with half the sugar, stirring constantly. Boil for 1 minute, remove from the heat, and stir in the chocolate and liqueur. Dot the surface with butter and leave until tepid. Meanwhile whisk the egg whites with a pinch of salt until they are thick, add the remaining sugar and continue to whisk until stiff and glossy. Stir the egg yolks, one by one, into the chocolate mixture, and then fold in a dollop of whites to lighten it. Fold in the rest of the whites and pour the mixture into the prepared dish. Bake in the centre of the oven for 35 minutes, or until the soufflé has risen, the top is brown and the centre still quivers. Serve immediately with the Crème Anglaise or lightly whipped cream.

51

# NUTCRACKER PUDDING

Preparation time: 25 minutes + 1 hour cooking — Serves 8

## For the pudding:

100 g (3½ oz) butter, softened, plus extra for greasing

100 g (3½ oz) vanilla caster sugar (page 8), plus extra for dusting

6 eggs, at room temperature, separated

100 g (3½ oz) unblanched almonds, ground

100 g (3½ oz) plain chocolate, refrigerated

2–3 tablespoons rum or brandy

oil for greasing

a pinch of salt

## For the cream:

300 ml (½ pint) double cream

2 tablespoons rum or brandy

1 tablespoon vanilla caster sugar

*A delicious steamed pudding with a lovely flavour from the nuts and chocolate. The inside is creamy which complements the steamed sponge. Serve it warm with brandy or rum flavoured whipped cream piled around its base.*

Butter and sugar a 1.1 kg (2½-pint) pudding basin or heatproof ring mould. Cream the butter until soft and then add the sugar and continue to beat until fluffy and light. Add the egg yolks, one at a time, blending each one in well before adding the next. Fold in the almonds. Grate the chocolate on the coarse side of a grater or in a rotary hand grinder. Fold it into the mixture along with the rum or brandy.

Whisk the egg whites with a pinch of salt until they are stiff. Fold a large spoonful of the whites into the chocolate mixture to lighten it before folding in the rest. Blend thoroughly without overmixing. Pour the batter into the basin and cover it with oiled and pleated foil tied securely with string.

Place a trivet in a pan large enough to hold the basin and fill it half-way with hot water. Place the basin on the trivet, cover the pan with a lid and simmer for 1 hour. Remove the basin from the water but leave the pudding in the mould for 5 minutes before turning it out on to a serving plate. Whip the cream, fold in the alcohol and sugar and spoon it around the pudding. Serve while the pudding is still warm.

*Chocolate Amaretti Filled Crêpes*

*Bitter Chocolate Soufflé*

*Nutcracker Pudding*

53

# CAKES AND PIES

## CHOCOLATE CHIFFON PIE

Preparation time: 40 minutes  
Serves 8–10  
+ 12 minutes cooking (optional)

**For the crust:**

150 g (5 oz) digestive biscuits

100 g (3½ oz) ground hazelnuts or almonds

75 g (3 oz) butter, melted

**For the filling:**

2 teaspoons gelatine

2 tablespoons cold water

2 large eggs (size 2), separated

150 g (5 oz) vanilla caster sugar (page 8)

250 ml (8 fl oz) milk

200 g (7 oz) plain chocolate, chopped

1 teaspoon instant coffee powder

300 ml (½ pint) double cream

a pinch of salt

**To decorate:**

grated chocolate or chocolate leaves (page 12)

**Oven temperature:**  
Gas Mark 4/180°C/350°F

*A tried-and-true American winner: chocolate chiffon floating on a crunchy crust.*

Preheat the oven. For the crust: crush the biscuits in a blender or processor until smooth. Add the nuts and butter and blend. Turn into a 23 cm (9-inch) flan dish and press the crumbs evenly over the bottom and sides of the plate. For a crisp crust bake for 10–12 minutes and when cool refrigerate until needed. You can also use the pie shell unbaked for a richer crust. Refrigerate until needed.

Place the gelatine and water in a cup for 5 minutes until the gelatine becomes spongy and then set the cup in hot water until the gelatine has dissolved.

Whisk the egg yolks with 125 g (4 oz) of the sugar until they are light and thick. Bring the milk to the boil, pour it over the egg yolks, whisking constantly, and then return the mixture to the saucepan. Stir with a wooden spoon over a low heat until the mixture thickens enough to coat the spoon. Do not allow it to boil or it will curdle. Remove the custard from the heat and stir in the gelatine, and then the chocolate and coffee. Set the bowl in iced water until it starts to thicken. Lightly whip the cream and fold it into the chocolate.

Whisk the egg whites with a pinch of salt until stiff, add the remaining sugar and whisk until the egg whites hold stiff peaks. Carefully fold the egg whites into the mixture ensuring that the chiffon is thoroughly blended without over-mixing. Turn it all into the prepared crust, piling it high in the centre. Cover the pie with cling film and refrigerate for at least 3 hours. The pie can be made 24 hours ahead of time and can also be frozen. Decorate it with grated chocolate or leaves before serving.

*Amaretto Chocolate Pie:* Replace the coffee with 4 tablespoons of amaretto liqueur. Add it after you have added the chocolate to the custard. Decorate the pie with amaretti biscuit crumbs.

## CHOCOLATE PECAN PIE

Preparation time: 30 minutes + 40 minutes baking + 30 minutes chilling                                Serves 8

**For the pastry:**

175 g (6 oz) plain flour

½ teaspoon salt

1 tablespoon caster sugar

1 teaspoon baking powder

75 g (3 oz) unsalted butter

1 egg yolk

3–4 tablespoons double cream

**For the filling:**

50 g (2 oz) butter

3 tablespoons cocoa powder

250 ml (8 fl oz) golden syrup

3 eggs

75 g (3 oz) soft dark brown sugar

2 tablespoons rum

175 g (6 oz) shelled pecan nuts

**Oven temperature:**
Gas Mark 4/180°C/350°F

*Pecan pie is one of the really great pies and chocolate pecan pie is even better. It is bound to be a success whenever it is served.*

To make the pastry: sift the flour, salt, sugar and baking powder together in a bowl. Cut the butter into small pieces and rub it into the mixture with your fingertips until the mixture has the texture of oatmeal. Blend the egg yolk with the cream and use a fork to stir it into the flour mixture. Form the dough into a round ball, wrap in cling film and refrigerate for 30 minutes. Roll out the dough and line a 24 cm (9½-inch) flan tin. Refrigerate while making the filling.

Place a baking sheet in the centre of the oven and preheat. For the filling: gently melt the butter in a saucepan and stir in the cocoa and the golden syrup. Using a medium-size bowl, lightly beat the eggs with the sugar and rum. Stir in the syrup mixture and the nuts. Pour the nut mixture into the pie shell and bake on the hot sheet for 35–40 minutes or until the filling is just set. Cover the pie with foil if the pastry becomes too dark. Serve warm or at room temperature with whipped cream or ice cream.

# CHOCOLATE PARIS-BREST

Preparation time: 30 minutes + 30 minutes baking
+ 1 hour cooling

Serves 12

### For the choux pastry:

150 g (5 oz) plain flour

100 g (3½ oz) lightly salted butter

250 ml (8 fl oz) water

5 eggs (size 2)

25 g (1 oz) flaked almonds

a pinch of salt

### For the filling:

Chocolate Crème Patissiere (page 87)

75 g (3 oz) Praline (page 87)

300 ml (½ pint) double cream

25 g (1 oz) cocoa powder

25 g (1 oz) icing sugar

### To decorate:

cocoa powder

*An impressive golden choux pastry ring, encrusted with almonds and filled with two different chocolate creams.*

Preheat the oven. Line two baking sheets with baking parchment. Draw a 20 cm (8-inch) circle on both papers. Sift the flour on to a square of baking parchment. Place the butter and water in a heavy-bottomed saucepan and slowly bring to the boil. Immediately remove from the heat and use a wooden spoon to beat in all the flour at once. Continue to beat over a very low heat until the mixture is smooth and pulls away from the sides of the saucepan. Take the saucepan off the heat and beat in four eggs, one at a time, mixing each one in thoroughly before adding the next. Mix the fifth egg in a small bowl and add only enough to make a mixture that just falls from the

*Heavenly Pie*

spoon. You may not need any of this fifth egg for the pastry, but it can be used for the egg glaze with a pinch of salt added.

Spoon the dough into a pastry bag fitted with a 1 cm (½-inch) plain tube. Pipe a ring on the line and then pipe a second ring just inside the first. Pipe a third ring on top, in the centre of the two other rings. Repeat on the other sheet. Brush the tops with egg glaze, prick the top with a fork and scatter the almonds over the top.

Bake the pastries for 30 minutes, until puffed, brown and crisp. Remove them from the oven to a wire rack and while the pastry is still hot, slice them in two with a sharp knife to allow the steam to escape. Once the pastries are completely cold, place them on a dish and cover to seal with cling film. An hour before serving, add the Praline to the Chocolate Crème Patissiere and spoon it into the bottom halves of the rings. Lightly whip the cream with the cocoa and sugar and pipe a zig zag line over the chocolate cream. Place the lids on top and sift a small amount of cocoa over the tops.

*Chocolate Pastry Fruit Tartlets*

*Chocolate Paris-Brest*

# HEAVENLY PIE

Preparation time: 25 minutes + 45 minutes baking        Serves 8
+ 30 minutes chilling

### For the pastry:

50 g (2 oz) skinned
hazelnuts

165 g (5½ oz) plain flour,
sifted

125 g (4 oz) lightly salted
butter, chilled and diced

25 g (1 oz) vanilla caster
sugar (page 8)

1 egg, lightly beaten

1–3 tablespoons iced water

### For the filling:

125 g (4 oz) plain
chocolate, chopped

50 g (2 oz) butter

2 large eggs (size 2)

100 g (3½ oz) vanilla
caster sugar

2 tablespoons plain flour,
sifted

4 tablespoons double cream

1½ tablespoons rum or
brandy (optional)

### To serve:

175 g (6 oz) double cream

1 tablespoon rum or brandy
(optional)

1 tablespoon icing sugar
(optional)

grated chocolate or chocolate
leaves (page 12)

### Oven temperatures:
Gas Mark 6/200°C/400°F
Gas Mark 5/190°C/375°F

*The texture of this pie is mousse-like and quite
heavenly with the crisp nut pastry.*

Place a baking sheet in the lower third of the
oven and preheat to the first setting. For the
pastry: use a coffee grinder or food processor to
grind the hazelnuts very finely. Place the ground
nuts and flour in a large bowl, add the butter and
sugar and work in with your fingertips to make a
crumb texture. Using a fork, mix in the egg and
if necessary enough water to form a dough.
Form the dough into a ball, wrap it in cling film
and refrigerate for 25–30 minutes. Roll the
dough out and line a 3.5 mm (1½-inch) deep
23 cm (9-inch) flan tin with a removable base.
Prick the base all over with a fork and then line it
with a crumpled piece of baking parchment
weighed down with dried beans. Place the flan
tin on the baking sheet and bake for 15 minutes,
lower the oven to the second setting, remove the
paper and beans and bake for a further 8–10
minutes. Place the pie case on a rack to cool,
leaving it in the tin, while you make the filling.
    For the filling: heat the oven to the second
setting again. Melt the chocolate and butter
together in the top of a double saucepan (page
10) and allow to cool. Beat the eggs and sugar
together in a large heatproof bowl set over hot
water. Whisk for about 10 minutes until the
mixture forms a ribbon trail when the whisk is
lifted. Sift the flour over the top and fold it in.
Pour the chocolate and butter mixture over the
top and fold it in, and then fold in the cream and
the alcohol, if used. Pour the pie filling into the
pastry case and bake on the hot baking sheet for
20 minutes. Remove to a rack to cool. Don't
worry if it cracks. Remove from the tin and
serve at room temperature or chilled with the
lightly whipped cream, flavoured with alcohol
and icing sugar if desired. The cream can also be

piped into rosettes on the pie. Decorate with grated chocolate or chocolate leaves.

# CHOCOLATE PASTRY FRUIT TARTLETS

Preparation time: 1 hour + 25 minutes baking     Makes 8 tartlets

*Delicious crisp chocolate tartlets piled high with colourful fruit are refreshing to both the palate and the eye.*

**For the pastry:**

*150 g (5 oz) lightly salted butter, cut into small pieces*

*50 g (2 oz) soft dark brown sugar*

*3 tablespoons cocoa powder*

*250 g (8 oz) plain flour*

*1 small egg white (size 4)*

**For the filling:**

*150 g (5 oz) redcurrant jelly*

*1 tablespoon water*

*150 ml (5 fl oz) double cream, lightly whipped*

*750 g (1½ lb) fresh fruit – strawberries, raspberries, kiwifruit, peaches, apricots or grapes*

**Oven temperature:**
*Gas Mark 4/180°C/350°F*

Preheat the oven. For the pastry: using a heavy-bottomed saucepan stir the butter, sugar and cocoa together over a low heat until blended. Remove from the heat the moment the butter has melted. Stir in the flour and then add just enough egg white to make a firm dough. Wrap the dough in cling film and refrigerate for 15 minutes. Roll out the dough between two sheets of baking parchment. Stamp out rounds 10 cm (4 inches) in diameter with a fluted cutter and line eight 7.5 cm (3-inch) tartlet tins. Prick the bases all over with a fork and refrigerate for 15 minutes before baking. Bake for 20–25 minutes. Cool on a rack before removing the tins.

For the filling: melt the redcurrant jelly with 1 tablespoon of water in the top of a double saucepan. Brush a thin layer of glaze over the bottom of the tartlets. This helps the pastry stay crisp. Spread a thin layer of cream over this and arrange the fruit over the top. Brush the fruit with a thin layer of the redcurrant glaze and serve.

*Note:* Apricot jam mixed with the juice of half a lemon and 2 tablespoons of water can be used in place of redcurrant jelly. This glaze is better for yellow and green fruit. Rub the hot jam through a strainer before using.

# TORTOISESHELL TORTE

Preparation time: 1¾ hours + 15 minutes cooking        Serves 12
+ 3 hours chilling

### For the sponge cake:

50 g (2 oz) self-raising flour

25 g (1 oz) cocoa powder

3 eggs

100 g (3½ oz) vanilla caster sugar (page 8), plus extra for dusting

6 tablespoons rum mixed with 6 tablespoons water

### For the apricot filling:

1 teaspoon gelatine

2 tablespoons + 150 ml (5 fl oz) cold water

175 g (6 oz) dried apricots

2 tablespoons granulated sugar

150 ml (5 fl oz) whipping cream

### For the chocolate cream:

175 g (6 oz) bitter dessert chocolate, chopped

150 g (5 oz) unsalted butter, cut into small pieces

2 eggs

75 g (3 oz) vanilla caster sugar

1–2 tablespoons rum (optional)

300 ml (½ pint) double cream, whipped

a pinch of salt

**Oven temperature:**
Gas Mark 6/200°C/400°F

*Though complicated, this cake is worth a little effort. Tiny slices of chocolate swiss roll make a tortoiseshell covering for this spectacular torte.*

Preheat the oven. For the sponge cake: line a 31 × 24 cm (12½ × 9½-inch) swiss roll tin with baking parchment. Sift the flour and cocoa together three times and set aside. Whisk the eggs and sugar in a heatproof bowl set over a pan of very hot water. Whisk until the mixture is very thick and leaves a ribbon trail when the whisk is lifted. Sift the flour-cocoa mixture over the eggs a quarter at a time, folding in with a large metal spoon after each addition. Pour the batter into the tin and spread level. Bake for 12–15 minutes. Remove from the oven, loosen the sides with a knife and turn the cake out on to a piece of baking parchment lightly sprinkled with caster sugar. Peel off the lining parchment, and then lay it back over the cake and replace the tin. Leave it for at least 10 minutes.

For the apricot filling: place the gelatine with 2 tablespoons of cold water in a small cup and leave it until it becomes spongy. Set the cup in very hot water and leave the gelatine to dissolve. Simmer the apricots with 150 ml (5 fl oz) of water in a saucepan, covered, until the apricots are soft and the water has evaporated. Blend the apricots with the sugar and the gelatine, add the cream and blend again.

To assemble the cake: slice the cake in two horizontally to make two thin layers. For best results use a long serrated knife and cut in a sawing motion. Spread the filling in a thin layer over the cut side of both cakes. Roll each slice tightly from both ends to make a double roll that meets in the centre. Cut through the centres, making four rolls (1). Refrigerate the rolls.

*Tortoiseshell Torte*

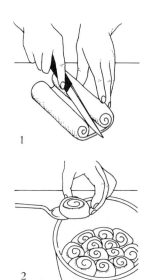

For the chocolate cream: melt the chocolate (page 10). Whisk in the butter and set it aside. Whisk the eggs, salt and sugar in a heatproof bowl set over a pan of hot water until the mixture is very thick and leaves a ribbon trail when the whisk is lifted. Use a metal spoon to fold in the chocolate mixture, rum, if you are using it, and then the whipped cream.

To assemble the Tortoiseshell Torte: line a 22 cm (8½-inch) cake tin 6 cm (2½ inches) deep with cling film, leaving an overlap at the top. Cut the rolls into 1 cm (½-inch) slices with a very sharp, thin knife. Lightly brush one side of a slice with the rum-water mixture and place it along the edge at the bottom of the tin, dipped side down. Continue with the other slices, working from edge to centre and then up the sides and arranging open ends of slices facing the same direction (2). Continue until the entire tin is covered. Try not to squeeze the slices or the filling may ooze and spoil the final tortoiseshell effect. Spoon the chocolate cream into the centre. Place any extra slices of the swiss roll on top of the filling. Cover with cling film and refrigerate for at least 3 hours or up to three days.

To serve: use the cling film to help remove the cake from the tin. Turn the dessert out on to a plate and serve it in thin slices.

## CHOCOLATE CAKE SUPREME

Preparation time: 1 hour + 35 minutes baking                    Serves 8–10

**For the cake:**

250 g (8 oz) plain chocolate, chopped

250 g (8 oz) unsalted butter, softened, plus extra for greasing

175 g (6 oz) vanilla caster sugar (page 8)

7 eggs, separated

75 g (3 oz) ground almonds

*This is a dream of a cake, dark and rich without being in the least heavy. It is perfectly matched by a luscious creamy chocolate frosting.*

Preheat the oven. Grease and line two 21 cm (8½-inch), shallow cake tins. Melt the chocolate (page 10). Cream the butter until light and then add the sugar and continue to beat until the mixture is fluffy. Beat in the egg yolks, one at a time, making sure each one is well blended before adding the next. Stir in the melted chocolate, ground almonds and liquid. Sift the

| | |
|---|---|
| 4 tablespoons coffee, rum or Cognac | flour with a pinch of salt three times and set aside. Whisk the egg whites with a pinch of salt until stiff peaks form. Fold a large spoon of the whites into the chocolate mixture to lighten it, then carefully fold in the rest. Sift the flour over the top of the mixture in two batches, carefully folding it in after each addition. Divide the batter between the two tins and bake for 35 minutes. Leave the cakes in the tins for 5 minutes before turning them out on to a rack to cool. |
| 125 g (4 oz) self-raising sponge flour | |
| 2 pinches of salt | |
| **For the frosting:** | |
| Chocolate Ganache (page 94) | |
| **Oven temperature:** Gas Mark 3/160°C/325°F | |

Make the Chocolate Ganache. Use it to sandwich the layers together and frost both the top and the sides with it.

## CHOCOLATE CHEESECAKE

Preparation time: 25 minutes + 1 hour baking + 6 hours chilling                    Serves 12–14

| | |
|---|---|
| 125 g (4 oz) ginger snap biscuits | *A thick, velvety American-style cheesecake with a ginger snap base.* |
| 40 g (1½ oz) butter, melted, plus extra for greasing | Preheat the oven. Grease a 20 cm (8-inch) diameter, 7.5 cm (3-inch) deep, springform cake tin and line the bottom with baking parchment. |
| 1 kg (2 lb) packaged cream cheese | Crush the biscuits in a food processor until smooth and then mix with the melted butter. Spoon the crust mixture into the tin and press over the bottom in an even layer. Using an electric mixer, beat the cream cheese until it is creamy. Mix in the sugar and then the eggs, one by one, being careful not to overmix. Stir the hot coffee into the cocoa and add to the cream cheese mixture. Pour the mixture into the prepared tin and bake for 1 hour. Cover loosely with foil towards the end of baking if necessary. When ready, the sides of the cake should be set but the centre still pudding-like. Cool the cake completely on a wire rack. Cover and refrigerate it until it is well chilled, about 6 hours. Remove the tin and transfer the cheesecake to a serving plate. Cut slices with a knife dipped in very hot water and then dried. |
| 250 g (8 oz) vanilla caster sugar (page 8) | |
| 4 eggs | |
| 6 tablespoons strong fresh-brewed coffee | |
| 50 g (2 oz) cocoa powder | |
| **Oven temperature:** Gas Mark 4/180°C/350°F | |

# MRS SCHWARZ'S NUSSTORTE

Preparation time: 45 minutes + 24 hours chilling
+ 45 minutes baking

Serves 8–10

**For the filling:**

450 ml (¾ pint) double cream

150 g (5 oz) plain chocolate

**For the cake:**

5 eggs, separated

175 g (6 oz) caster sugar

150 g (5 oz) walnuts, ground

25 g (1 oz) biscuit crumbs, such as Marie

1 tablespoon cocoa powder

1 tablespoon powdered instant coffee

a dash of rum or lemon juice

butter for greasing

flour for dusting

*Mrs Schwarz left Vienna for England in 1937 with her husband, young children and cook. When the cook returned home at the outbreak of war, Mrs Schwarz took over the kitchen. Although she had no practical experience at that point, she did have her Austrian cookbooks and a beautiful collection of cake moulds that had been part of her trousseau. Using them ever since, she has become an inspired baker whose cakes are among the best I have ever tasted.*

For the filling: place the cream and the chocolate in the top of a double saucepan set over boiling water and stir until the chocolate has dissolved. Cool and then cover the cream with cling film and refrigerate overnight. Whip like ordinary

*Chocolate Cloud Cake*

*Mrs Schwarz's Nusstorte*

6 tablespoons redcurrant
jelly

a pinch of salt

**Oven temperature:**
Gas Mark 4/180°C/350°F

cream before using.

For the cake: preheat the oven. Whisk the egg
yolks and sugar together with an electric mixer
until light and thick, several minutes. Using a
large metal spoon fold in the nuts, biscuit
crumbs, cocoa, coffee and rum or lemon juice.
Whisk the egg whites with a pinch of salt until
stiff peaks form and then carefully fold into the
egg yolk mixture. Pour the batter into a greased
and floured 23–24 cm (9–9½-inch) springform
tin and bake for 45 minutes. Cool the cake in the
tin for 5 minutes before turning it out on to a
wire rack to cool.

When the cake is cool slice it into two discs.
Heat the redcurrant jelly gently to melt it and
brush a good coating over the cut layers. Spread
some of the filling over this and sandwich the
cake together. Brush the top of the cake with a
layer of the jelly; then cover both sides and top
with the remaining filling.

*Orange Devil's Food Cake*

# CHOCOLATE CLOUD CAKE

Preparation time: 45 minutes + 40 minutes baking          Serves 8–10

### For the cake:

100 g (3½ oz) plain flour

40 g (1½ oz) cocoa powder

½ teaspoon baking powder

4 eggs

150 g (5 oz) vanilla caster sugar (page 8)

40 g (1½ oz) unsalted butter, plus extra for greasing

a pinch of salt

### For the rum syrup:

75 g (3 oz) granulated sugar

3 tablespoons water

7 tablespoons rum

### For the frosting:

150 g (5 oz) plain chocolate

3 eggs, separated

75 g (3 oz) unsalted butter, cut into small pieces

1 teaspoon rum

a pinch of salt

### To decorate:

chocolate and white chocolate curls (page 12)

### Oven temperature:
Gas Mark 4/180°C/350°F

*This is an amazing cake. Both the cake and frosting are incredibly light and airy yet have a scrumptious flavour and texture.*

Preheat the oven. Grease a 23 cm (9-inch) cake tin and line the bottom with baking parchment. Sift the flour, cocoa, baking powder and salt together three times. Break the eggs into a large heatproof bowl, preferably a copper one, and set it over a pan of very hot but not boiling water. Using an electric hand-held beater, whisk the eggs with the caster sugar for 6–8 minutes, until the mixture has doubled in volume and is thick enough to leave a ribbon trail when the whisk is lifted. Melt the butter over a gentle heat. Sift the dry ingredients over the egg mixture a third at a time, folding in each batch carefully with a large metal spoon and then fold in the melted butter. Pour the mixture into the prepared tin and bake in a preheated oven for 35–40 minutes or until the cake springs back when lightly pressed. Leave the cake in the tin for a few minutes before turning out. Slip a knife around the edge of the cake and turn it out on to a rack to cool.

Make the rum syrup while the cake is baking. Heat the sugar with 3 tablespoons of water to dissolve and then bring to the boil. Remove from the heat and when the syrup has cooled, add the rum.

For the frosting, melt the chocolate in the top of a double saucepan (page 10). Remove from the heat and beat in the egg yolks, one by one. Stir the butter and rum into the chocolate mixture. Whisk the egg whites with a pinch of salt until just stiff. Using a large metal spoon, fold a dollop of the whites into the cooled chocolate mixture to lighten it and then fold in the rest of the whites.

Split the cake into two discs. Dab the rum syrup over the cut side of each cake layer. Layer the discs with some of the frosting and spread

the remainder on the top and sides of the cake.
Decorate the cake with white and plain chocolate
curls. Any remaining rum syrup can be served
separately with the cake.

# ORANGE DEVIL'S FOOD CAKE

Preparation time: 1 hour + 30 minutes baking                    Serves 8–10

*This dark, rich cake, layered and frosted with a fluffy orange icing, is quite irresistible.*

**For the cake:**

50 g (2 oz) cocoa powder

175 ml (6 fl oz) boiling water

175 g (6 oz) butter, softened, plus extra for greasing

300 g (10 oz) soft dark brown sugar

3 eggs

300 g (10 oz) plain flour

1½ teaspoons bicarbonate of soda

¼ teaspoon baking powder

175 ml (6 fl oz) soured cream

**For the icing:**

300 g (10 oz) caster sugar

2 egg whites

1 tablespoon lemon juice

the grated rind of 1 orange

4 tablespoons concentrated frozen orange juice

**Oven temperature:**
*Gas Mark 4/180°C/350°F*

Preheat the oven. For the cake: grease two 23 cm (9-inch) shallow cake tins and line the bottoms with baking parchment. In a small bowl mix the cocoa and the boiling water until smooth. Cream the butter in a large bowl and slowly add the sugar, beating until light and fluffy. Add the eggs, one at a time, beating well after each addition. When the cocoa mixture has cooled to a hand-hot temperature, stir it into the creamed mixture. Sift the flour with the bicarbonate of soda and baking powder twice. Add this to the cocoa mixture in several batches, alternating it with the soured cream. Pour the batter into the prepared tins and bake for about 30 minutes. Cool the cakes in the tins for 5 minutes before turning them out on to wire racks to cool completely.

For the icing: place all the ingredients in the top of a double saucepan set over simmering water. Whisk with a hand-held electric beater or a wire whisk until the mixture thickens and forms soft peaks when the beater is lifted. Remove the double saucepan from the heat and continue to beat until the icing is at the right consistency to spread. Sandwich the cake layers with some of the icing and spread the rest over the top and sides.

# CHOCOLATE HAZELNUT MERINGUE CAKE

Preparation time: 25 minutes + 45 minutes baking     Serves 10

*butter for greasing*

*125 g (4 oz) hazelnuts*

*4 egg whites*

*275 g (9 oz) caster sugar*

*25 g (1 oz) cocoa powder*

*300 ml (½ pint) double cream*

*625 g (1¼ lb) fresh or frozen raspberries, thawed if frozen*

*a pinch of salt*

**Oven temperatures:**
*Gas Mark 4/180°C/350°F*
*Gas Mark 3/160°C/325°F*

*You may already know how fabulous hazelnut meringues with raspberries taste, but try chocolate hazelnut meringues and raspberries: they are even more sensational.*

Preheat the oven to the first setting. Grease two 20 cm (8-inch) sandwich tins and line the bottoms with baking parchment. Spread the nuts on a baking sheet and bake them for about 8 minutes, or until the nuts are lightly toasted. Rub the nuts together in a towel to remove most of the skins. Grind the nuts in a processor or blender. Lower the oven to the second setting. Whisk the egg whites with the salt until stiff, add the sugar, a little at a time, and continue to whisk until the mixture forms stiff, glossy peaks. Sift the cocoa over the top and fold in, then fold in the nuts. Divide the meringue between the tins and smooth the tops with a palette knife. Bake for 45 minutes; the tops will be crisp but the insides still soft. Leave the meringues in the tins for 10 minutes before turning them out on to a rack to cool; then peel off the paper.

Whip the cream. Sandwich the meringues with half of the cream and raspberries and use the remaining cream and raspberries for the top. Keep the meringue cake in the refrigerator to facilitate cutting.

*Note:* If you are storing meringues for any length of time, it is prudent to dry them off in a turned-off oven for 1–2 hours after baking.

# UPSIDE-DOWN CAKE

Preparation time: 30 minutes + 30 minutes cooking                    Serves 8

### For the cake:

*100 g (3½ oz) bitter or best quality plain chocolate*

*75 g (3 oz) unsalted butter, cut into pieces, plus extra for greasing*

*3 eggs*

*150 g (5 oz) vanilla caster sugar (page 8)*

*40 g (1½ oz) plain flour*

*a pinch of salt*

### For the glaze:

*75 g (3 oz) plain chocolate*

*25 g (1 oz) butter*

*1 tablespoon milk*

**Oven temperature:**
*Gas Mark 4/180°C/350°F*

*This delectable cake forms a light crust when it is baked which provides a base when the cake is turned upside-down. The chocolate glaze wraps it up into a very special treat. It makes a perfect dinner party dessert.*

Preheat the oven. Grease a 20 cm (8-inch), shallow cake tin and line the bottom with baking parchment. For the cake: stir the chocolate and butter together in the top of a double saucepan, set over barely simmering water until they are just blended. Remove the chocolate from the heat and set it aside. Whisk the eggs, salt and sugar together in a large heatproof bowl, set over hot water, until the mixture forms a ribbon trail when the whisk is lifted, about 8 minutes. Sift the flour over the top and fold it in with a large metal spoon. Pour the chocolate mixture over the top and fold it in. Turn the batter into the cake tin and bake for 25–30 minutes, or until the cake is risen and has a light crust. Place it on a rack and leave it in the tin for 10 minutes. Don't worry if the cake deflates a little in the middle. Slip a knife around the edge and turn it out on to a plate and allow to cool.

For the glaze: melt all the glaze ingredients together in a double saucepan and spread over the cooled cake.

# SMALL CAKES AND COOKIES

## CHOCOLATE PRETZELS

Preparation time: 40 minutes + 1 hour chilling
+ 12 minutes baking

Makes 28 pretzels

*125 g (4 oz) unsalted butter, cut into small pieces, plus extra for greasing*

*125 g (4 oz) vanilla caster sugar (page 8)*

*1 egg*

*3 tablespoons cocoa powder*

*165 g (5½ oz) plain flour, plus extra for dusting*

*1 egg white for glazing*

*coarse or granulated sugar for coating*

*a big pinch of salt*

**Oven temperature:**
*Gas Mark 5/190°C/375°F*

*In the United States, especially New York or Boston, pretzels are immensely popular. On many street corners you can buy them fresh, hot, and chewy from a vendor. For a biscuit with a difference, chilled chocolate biscuit dough can be shaped into a small pretzel shape. Pretzels are made by rolling small balls of dough into long ropes and twisting them into the traditional shape. They look even more realistic with flecks of sugar to resemble salt.*

Cream the butter, either in a processor or by hand. Add the sugar and mix until fluffy, and then mix in the whole egg, cocoa, flour and salt. Form the dough into a ball, wrap it in cling film and refrigerate it for 1 hour, or freeze for 30 minutes. Preheat the oven. Work on a lightly floured surface with lightly floured hands. Divide the dough into 28 small balls and roll each in turn into a long rope. With each rope, form a loop with the two ends facing you. Twist the ends and fold back on to the circle, pressing in to make a pretzel shape. Place it on a greased baking sheet. Refrigerate while you make the rest. Remove the baking sheet from the refrigerator and brush the pretzels with lightly beaten egg white. Scatter sugar over the tops and bake them for 12 minutes. Remove the pretzels to wire racks to cool. Keep them in an airtight container when cold.

# CHOCOLATE HAZELNUT TUILES

Preparation time: 45 minutes + 40 minutes baking

Makes about 16 tuiles

75 g (3 oz) hazelnuts

100 g (3½ oz) vanilla caster sugar (page 8)

50 g (2 oz) unsalted butter, plus extra for greasing

5 teaspoons cocoa powder

3 tablespoons double cream

2 large egg whites (size 2)

40 g (1½ oz) plain flour, plus extra for dusting

2 tablespoons rum

a pinch of salt

**Oven temperatures:**
Gas Mark 4/180°C/350°F
Gas Mark 7/220°C/425°F

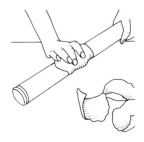

*These thin, crisp, deliciously flavoured tuiles can be shaped as cups to make edible ice-cream containers.*

Preheat the oven to the first setting. Toast the nuts on a baking sheet for 10 minutes. Rub them in a tea towel to remove most of the skins. Chop one third of the nuts and set them aside. Finely grind the remaining nuts with the sugar in a blender or processor. Preheat the oven to the second setting. Cream the butter with a wooden spoon, and then blend in the sugar-nut mixture, salt, cocoa and cream. Add the egg whites stirring only enough to blend. Sift and fold in the flour and lastly the rum. Butter and flour a baking sheet. Mark circles 11 cm (4½ inches) in diameter about 5 cm (2 inches) apart. A bowl turned upside down and gently rotated can be used on the buttered and floured baking sheet. Place 1 scant tablespoon of the batter in the centre of each circle and spread it out thinly with the back of the spoon to cover the circle. Sprinkle a pinch of the reserved nuts over the top. Bake for about 5 minutes, or until the edges are just beginning to darken. Remove the tuiles, one at a time, with a spatula and place them over a rolling pin, or in a cup, or shape around a metal or paper horn. If possible, set the baking sheet on the open oven door to keep the tuiles warm and pliable. Work quickly as the tuiles crisp in a few seconds. Wait for the oven to reach the correct temperature before baking another batch. Store carefully in an airtight container.

*Note:* cone-shaped biscuits can be used as ice cream containers. Also, their edges can be dipped in chocolate and the cones filled with whipped cream or Chocolate Ganache (page 94).

# CHOCOLATE DIPPED MERINGUES

Preparation time: 15 minutes
+ 2 hours baking

Makes 18–20 double meringues

| |
|---|
| *4 egg whites* |
| *200 g (7 oz) vanilla caster sugar (page 8)* |
| *150 g (5 oz) plain chocolate* |
| *1 teaspoon instant coffee powder* |
| *1 tablespoon hot water* |
| *250 ml (8 fl oz) double cream* |
| **Oven temperature:** *Gas Mark ½ / 130°C / 250°F* |

*Almost everyone loves meringues and these are particularly nice with their dark chocolate edge and coffee cream filling. The mixture can also be spooned, rather than piped, into mounds and baked.*

Preheat the oven and line two baking sheets with baking parchment. If you like, cut an oval shape out of a card about 3.5 cm (1½ inches) in diameter to use as a guide. Use it to trace shapes in pencil on the baking parchment, leaving space between each for spreading. Turn the paper over and stick the corners down with a dot of the meringue.

Whisk the egg whites until they form soft peaks and then whisk in the sugar, a few table-spoons at a time, until thick and very stiff. Spoon the meringue into a pastry bag fitted with a medium-size nozzle. Pipe the meringue back and forth following the outline. Bake the meringues for 2 hours, until they are dry and crisp. Leave them to cool slightly and then transfer them to a wire rack to cool completely.

Melt the chocolate (page 10). Dip the bottom of each meringue shell in chocolate and place the dipped-side down on baking parchment to set. Dissolve the coffee in the water, allow to cool then add to the cream and whip. Sandwich two meringues together generously with the cream and place them on their sides in paper cases.

*Chocolate Pretzels*

*Chocolate Hazelnut Tuiles filled with Chocolate Ganache*

*Chocolate Dipped Meringues*

73

# CHOCOLATE NUT REFRIGERATOR COOKIES

Preparation and cooking time: 25 minutes     Makes about 18 cookies
+ 12 hours chilling

200 g (7 oz) plain flour

½ teaspoon bicarbonate of soda

25 g (1 oz) cocoa powder

150 g (5 oz) lightly salted butter, plus extra for greasing

150 g (5 oz) dark muscovado sugar

25 g (1 oz) granulated sugar

1 egg

125 g (4 oz) walnuts, chopped very finely

**Oven temperature:**
Gas Mark 5/190°C/375°F

*One of the very best cookies, short, crisp and deliciously flavoured. The dough is rolled, chilled then sliced very thinly to bake.*

Sift the flour, bicarbonate of soda and cocoa together and set it aside. Cream the butter with both sugars until light and fluffy and then gradually stir in the egg. Fold in the flour and the chopped nuts. Use lightly floured hands to roll the dough into a sausage shape 5 cm (2 inches) in diameter. Wrap it tightly in cling film and chill for 12 hours or longer.

Preheat the oven. Use a very sharp, thin knife to cut the dough into thin slices. Place the cookies on greased baking sheets and bake for 8–10 minutes. Remove the cookies with a spatula while they are still hot and place them on a flat surface to cool. Store them in an airtight tin.

# BROWNIES

Preparation and cooking time: 40 minutes         Makes 16

125 g (4 oz) butter, plus extra for greasing

40 g (1½ oz) cocoa powder

2 eggs

250 g (8 oz) vanilla caster sugar (page 8)

50 g (2 oz) self-raising flour

75 g (3 oz) chopped walnuts

**Oven temperature:**
Gas Mark 4/180°C/350°F

*No book on chocolate would be complete without a recipe for brownies, the all-time American favourite.*

Preheat the oven. Grease a 20 cm (8-inch) square shallow cake tin and line the bottom with baking parchment. Gently melt the butter in a small saucepan and then stir in the cocoa until it is blended in and set the mixture aside. In a medium-size bowl, beat the eggs and sugar together until light, and then add the cocoa mixture to it. Sift the flour over the top of the mixture and gently fold it in with a large metal spoon. Add the nuts and turn the batter into the prepared tin. Bake in the centre of the oven for 25–35 minutes. Do not overcook; brownies firm up as they cool. Leave in the tin until cool before cutting into 5 cm (2-inch) squares and removing them from the tin. The brownies should be quite soft and moist inside.

# BISHOP'S BREAD

Preparation time: 20 minutes + 50 minutes baking        Makes 1 loaf

*100 g (3½ oz) self-raising flour*

*25 g (1 oz) cornflour*

*¼ teaspoon baking powder*

*140 g (4½ oz) lightly salted butter, plus extra for greasing*

*140 g (4½ oz) vanilla caster sugar (page 8), plus extra for dusting*

*2 eggs, at room temperature*

*25 g (1 oz) sultanas*

*25 g (1 oz) chopped walnuts*

*grated rind of ½ lemon*

*40 g (1½ oz) plain chocolate, cut into pea-size pieces*

**To serve:**

*icing sugar for dusting*

**Oven temperature:**
*Gas Mark 4/180°C/350°F*

*This is the perfect cake to serve with tea although I imagine that it is more often enjoyed with coffee in Austria, where it originates. It has a beautiful texture, light yet buttery with just a hint of chocolate, lemon, nuts and sultanas. This is another of Mrs Schwarz's recipes.*

Preheat the oven. Butter and sugar a small Balmoral or plain 500 g (1 lb) loaf tin. Sift the self-raising flour, cornflour and baking powder together three times. Beat the butter until it is soft and creamy then add the sugar and beat until fluffy. Lightly whisk the eggs, then gradually stir them into the butter mixture. It is important that the eggs are at room temperature as they then blend better and will not curdle the butter. Carefully fold the dry ingredients into the mixture, by thirds, using a large metal spoon. Be careful not to overmix. Fold in the sultanas, walnuts, lemon rind and chocolate. Pour the batter into the prepared tin and bake it in the centre of the oven for 45–50 minutes. Cool the cake in the tin for 5 minutes before turning it out on to a rack to finish cooling. Dust with icing sugar before serving. Keep wrapped in foil for storing.

# ITALIAN CHOCOLATE ALMOND BISCUITS

Preparation time: 25 minutes + 45 minutes baking          Makes about 48

125 g (4 oz) unblanched almonds

250 g (8 oz) plain flour plus extra for dusting

100 g (3½ oz) vanilla caster sugar (page 8)

1 teaspoon bicarbonate of soda

2 eggs

75 g (3 oz) plain chocolate

butter for greasing

1 egg white

a pinch of salt

**Oven temperatures:**
Gas Mark 5/190°C/375°F
Gas Mark 1/140°C/275°F

*In Northern Italy these crunchy very dry biscuits are served accompanied by a glass of Vin Santo. The biscuits are dunked in the sweet wine which softens and flavours them beautifully. If you can't find a Vin Santo try serving them with a Sauternes for an unusual dessert.*

Preheat the oven to the first setting. Lightly toast the almonds in the oven for about 10 minutes. Leave the oven on. When they have cooled chop half of the nuts very coarsely and set aside. Finely grind the other half in a processor or blender. Mix the flour, sugar, salt, bicarbonate of soda and ground nuts in a large bowl. Make a well in the centre and break in the eggs. Stir from the centre to form a rough dough. Melt the chocolate in the top of a double saucepan (page 10), and stir into the dough. Knead the dough on a floured surface until well blended and then work in the chopped almonds. Divide the dough into three equal parts and roll them into sausage shapes 2.5 cm (1 inch) in diameter. Place them on a buttered and floured baking sheet, leaving room to spread. Beat the egg white slightly in a small bowl and brush over the rolls. Bake for 20 minutes. Remove from the oven and cut the cylinders at an angle with a very sharp knife into 1 cm (½-inch) slices. Place the slices back on the baking sheet, lower the oven to the second setting and bake for 25 minutes more. Cool the biscuits on a rack before storing them in an airtight tin.

*Italian Chocolate Almond Biscuits*
*Florentines*

# FLORENTINES

Preparation and cooking time: 40 minutes          Makes 2 dozen

40 g (1½ oz) salted butter, plus extra for greasing

5 tablespoons double cream

50 g (2 oz) caster sugar

100 g (3½ oz) blanched almonds, 65 g (2½ oz) chopped finely and the rest flaked

40 g (1½ oz) candied orange peel, chopped finely

25 g (1 oz) plain flour

a pinch of salt

**For the topping:**

150 g (5 oz) plain chocolate, chopped

**Oven temperature:**
Gas Mark 4/180°C/350°F

*These are among the nicest of all biscuits and not at all difficult to make despite their delicate appearance.*

Preheat the oven. Melt the butter, cream and sugar together and slowly bring to boiling point. Remove the saucepan from the heat and add the almonds and orange peel. When these are blended stir in the flour and salt. Drop rounded teaspoons of the mixture on to a greased baking sheet, leaving space between each one for spreading. Flatten the mixture with a wet fork and bake for about 12 minutes, or until browned at the edges. Cool the biscuits slightly on the sheet before removing them with a spatula to a flat surface to cool.

For the topping: melt the chocolate (page 10). Use a palette knife to spread the undersides of the biscuits with the chocolate. Before the chocolate has set, mark wavy lines with a confectioner's comb or a serrated knife.

# CHOCOLATE MACAROONS

Preparation time: 35 minutes + 12 minutes baking     Makes 2½ dozen

125 g (4 oz) unblanched almonds

65 g (2½ oz) plain chocolate

125 g (4 oz) vanilla caster sugar (page 8)

¼ teaspoon almond essence

1 tablespoon cocoa powder

2 egg whites

icing sugar for dusting

**Oven temperatures:**
Gas Mark 4/180°C/350°F
Gas Mark 6/200°C/400°F

*These are lovely macaroons, crisp on the outside and chewy inside.*

Preheat the oven to the first setting. Place the almonds on a baking sheet and bake them for 8 minutes. This will bring out more flavour. Remove them from the oven and leave to cool. Melt the chocolate in the top of a double saucepan (page 10) and set aside. Place the cooled almonds in a processor or blender and grind them to a fine powder. Mix them with the caster sugar, almond essence, melted chocolate, cocoa and one egg white. Blend together adding just enough of the second egg white to form a soft paste. Line a baking sheet with baking parchment and preheat the oven to the second setting. Use

78

your hands to shape the dough into balls the size of walnuts. Place them on the paper and flatten slightly. Brush each ball with a little water and dust them with a little sifted icing sugar. Bake for about 12 minutes or until just firm. Remove the baking tray from the oven. If necessary lift one end of the paper and pour about half a cup of water under the paper. The hot baking tray will make the water turn to steam under the macaroons and will enable them to come away from the paper with ease. Cool them on a rack and store them in an airtight container.

# CHOCOLATE SHORTBREAD

Preparation and cooking time: 40 minutes + 1½ hours chilling

Makes about 20

275 g (9 oz) plain flour

25 g (1 oz) cocoa powder

¼ teaspoon salt

250 g (8 oz) unsalted butter, softened

150 g (5 oz) icing sugar, sifted, plus extra for dusting

1 teaspoon vanilla essence (if available; do not substitute vanilla flavouring)

butter for greasing if necessary

**Oven temperature:**
Gas Mark 3/ 160°C/ 325°F

*Shorter than short, these literally melt in the mouth.*

Sift the flour, cocoa and salt together and set aside. Cream the butter, sugar and vanilla extract together and then slowly incorporate the flour mixture. This can also be done in a food processor by first blending the dry ingredients together and then adding the vanilla if available, and the butter, cut into small pieces, and processing until a dough is formed.

Roll the dough out between two sheets of cling film until it is about 1 cm (½-inch) thick. Place the dough, still in the cling film, on a flat surface, such as a baking sheet, and refrigerate for 1½ hours or until firm.

Preheat the oven. Remove the top piece of cling film and cut out 3.5 cm (1½-inch) rounds with a pastry cutter. Place them on well greased baking sheets or baking sheets lined with baking parchment. Bake the shortbread for 15 minutes and then cool the biscuits on a wire rack. When cool, dust the shortbread with icing sugar. These biscuits keep very well if stored in an airtight container.

# MUFFINS AU CHOCOLAT

Preparation time: 20 minutes + 25 minutes baking          Makes 10

*125 g (4 oz) lightly salted butter, plus extra for greasing*

*75 g (3 oz) granulated sugar*

*25 g (1 oz) dark brown sugar*

*2 eggs*

*200 g (7 oz) self-raising sponge flour or self-raising flour*

*7 tablespoons milk*

*65 g (2½ oz) plain chocolate, cut into 1 cm (½ inch) pieces*

**Oven temperature:**
*Gas Mark 5/190°C/375°F*

*These are an American version of Pain au chocolat; they make delicious snacks.*

Preheat the oven. Grease bun tins that have 3.5 cm (1½-inch) or 2.5 cm (1-inch) deep wells or line the wells with paper cases.

Cream the butter until it is fluffy, then work in both sugars until you have a light mixture. Gradually incorporate the eggs. Sift the flour twice. Add it to the butter mixture in several batches, alternating it with the milk. Divide half of the mixture between the bun wells. Place two or three pieces of chocolate over the mixture and cover with a spoonful of the batter. Half-fill any empty wells with water for even baking. Bake for about 25 minutes for the deeper wells or 22 minutes for the shallower wells or until the muffins have risen and are lightly coloured. Leave the muffins in the tins for a few minutes before turning them out on to a rack to cool. These muffins store well if kept in an airtight container.

*Muffins au Chocolat*
*Fudge Fingers*
*White Chocolate Chip Cookies*

# FUDGE FINGERS

Preparation time: 15 minutes
+ 30 minutes chilling

Makes about 20 fingers

65 g (2½ oz) hazelnuts

150 g (5 oz) plain chocolate

150 g (5 oz) unsalted butter

150 g (5 oz) digestive
biscuits

a good pinch of salt

**Oven temperature:**
Gas Mark 4/180°C/350°F

*Dense and rich, these are like bars of fudge studded with chopped biscuits and nuts.*

Preheat the oven. Spread the nuts on a baking tray and bake until the nuts are lightly toasted. Rub the nuts in a cloth to remove most of the skins; then chop roughly. Melt the chocolate, butter and salt together in the top of a double saucepan. Cut the biscuits into 1 cm (½-inch) pieces. Mix the biscuits and nuts into the chocolate and turn the mixture into an 18 cm (7-inch) square tin lined with baking parchment. Press the mixture into a smooth layer and refrigerate for 30 minutes. Cut into fingers. Store in an airtight container in the refrigerator or a cool place.

# WHITE CHOCOLATE CHIP COOKIES

Preparation time: 30 minutes + 15 minutes baking

Makes about 36

125 g (4 oz) lightly salted
butter, softened, plus extra
for greasing

40 g (1½ oz) vanilla caster
sugar (page 8)

65 g (2½ oz) soft dark
brown sugar

1 egg

125 g (4 oz) plain flour

½ teaspoon bicarbonate of
soda

150 g (5 oz) white
chocolate, cut into pea-size
pieces

50 g (2 oz) chopped walnuts

**Oven temperature:**
Gas Mark 4/180°C/350°F

*Crisp cookies studded with nuggets of white chocolate are a must for white chocolate fans. If you prefer dark chocolate use plain chocolate for the recipe and you will have a delicious, if more conventional, treat.*

Preheat the oven and grease two baking sheets. Cream the butter and the two sugars together until light and fluffy. Lightly mix the egg and gradually beat it into the creamed mixture. Sift the flour and bicarbonate of soda together and stir it into the mixture. Finally stir in the chocolate bits and the walnuts.

Spoon heaped teaspoons of the mixture on to the prepared sheets, leaving room to spread. Bake for 10–15 minutes, or until the cookies are light brown. Remove with a spatula while they are hot and place on any flat surface to cool. They will become crisp as they cool. Store them in an airtight container.

# DOUBLE CHOCOLATE SQUARES

Preparation and cooking time: 50 minutes          Makes about 20 squares

**For the cake:**

100 g (3½ oz) plain flour

40 g (1½ oz) cocoa powder

½ teaspoon baking powder

4 eggs

150 g (5 oz) vanilla caster sugar (page 8)

40 g (1½ oz) unsalted butter

a pinch of salt

Chocolate Butter Cream (page 87)

**For the icing:**

250 g (8 oz) plain chocolate

4 tablespoons water

50 g (2 oz) lightly salted butter, cut into pieces

**Oven temperature:**
Gas Mark 4/180°C/350°F

*Small squares of chocolate cake are filled with a thick layer of butter cream and covered with dark chocolate. They are perfect for a special tea party and can be sliced and served with a scoop of vanilla ice cream for a yummy dessert.*

Preheat the oven. Line a 34 × 24 cm (13½ × 9½-inch) shallow tin with baking parchment. Sift the flour, cocoa, baking powder and salt together three times. Break the eggs into a large heatproof bowl, preferably a copper one, and set it over a pan of very hot but not boiling water. Using an electric hand-held beater, whisk the eggs with the caster sugar for 6–8 minutes, until the mixture has doubled in volume and is thick enough to leave a ribbon trail when the whisk is lifted. Melt the butter over a low heat. Sift the dry ingredients over the mixture a third at a time, folding in each batch carefully with a large metal spoon, and then fold in the melted butter. Pour the mixture into the prepared tin and bake for 15–20 minutes until well risen and springy to the touch. Meanwhile make the Chocolate Butter Cream. When the cake is ready, slip a knife around the edge of the cake, turn it out on to a rack and peel away the paper. When the cake is cool cut it in two lengthways and thickly spread the butter cream over one half and sandwich it with the other half.

For the icing: melt the chocolate and water in the top of a double saucepan (page 10). Stir in the butter and allow the icing to thicken slightly as it cools. Spread the icing over the cake with a palette knife while the icing is still slightly warm. Refrigerate the cake until the icing is set and you are serving the cake. Cut it into 5 cm (2-inch) squares with a long, sharp knife dipped in hot water and dried.

# SWEETS AND SAUCES

## CHOCOLATE ARTICHOKE

Preparation time: 1¼ hours + 1 hour setting          Makes 1 artichoke

*500 g (1 lb) plain chocolate*

*2 tablespoons sunflower or groundnut oil*

*4–5 drops of oil of peppermint (available at chemists)*

*a globe artichoke*

**To assemble the chocolate artichoke:**

*25 g (1 oz) caster sugar*

*25 g (1 oz) butter*

*2 tablespoons water*

*50 g (2 oz) icing sugar, sifted*

*25 g (1 oz) cocoa powder, sifted*

*a 6.5 cm (2½-inch) square piece of cake*

*A chocolate artichoke is certain to provide a talking point and is an amusing finale for a special dinner. The leaves can be pulled off and eaten as after-dinner mints. It looks very difficult to make but is surprisingly easy and fun to do.*

Melt the chocolate in the top of a double saucepan (page 10). Stir in the sunflower or groundnut oil and the peppermint oil. Do not use cake covering as it is unsuitable. Allow the chocolate to drop to blood temperature before dipping. Peel the leaves off the artichoke, discarding any dirty or damaged ones, and dip the outside of the leaves in the chocolate. Shake any excess chocolate back into the pan and lay the chocolate leaves on a flat surface covered in baking parchment. Try and keep them in the order that you have removed them from the artichoke. Leave them in a cool room for 2–3 hours before carefully peeling off the real artichoke leaves. Don't worry if you break a few because you won't need the entire amount.

Dissolve the caster sugar in the butter and water over a low heat. Remove from the heat and stir in the icing sugar and cocoa. Cut the cake into a cone-shape. Cover the cake with some of the cooled icing, reserving the rest for attaching the leaves. Break about a third of the bottom off seven to eight of the inner centre leaves. Stick them carefully into the upper sides of the cone. Follow the same order as the real artichoke leaves. Stick the next layers of chocolate leaves just below, leaving them whole. Continue working around the cone using extra icing to help make the leaves stick. You won't be able to fit in all the leaves. Place the finished artichoke on a serving dish and leave in a cool place to set, about 1 hour.

*Chocolate Artichoke* ➤

*White Artichoke:* replace the plain chocolate with white chocolate and omit the sunflower or groundnut oil and the oil of peppermint. Also omit the cocoa powder from the icing.

# CRÈME ANGLAISE

Preparation time: 10 minutes                    Makes 350 ml (12 fl oz)

*300 ml (½ pint) milk*

*½ vanilla pod, split in two*

*3 egg yolks*

*25 g (1 oz) vanilla caster sugar (page 8)*

*This custard sauce goes beautifully with many chocolate desserts. For a thicker creamier sauce, fold in 150 ml (5 fl oz) of lightly whipped cream.*

Bring the milk with the vanilla pod to just below boiling point. Whisk the egg yolks with the sugar until thick and light; then whisk in the hot milk. Return the mixture to the pan and cook over a very low heat, stirring constantly with a wooden spoon, until the mixture thickens slightly. Your finger should leave a clear trail when drawn across the back of the spoon. Do not allow the custard to boil or it will curdle. Strain it into a bowl, cool and then refrigerate it. Wash and dry the vanilla pod and use it for vanilla sugar. The custard will thicken a little more as it cools. It can be kept for two to three days if refrigerated.

# CRÈME PATISSIERE

Preparation time: 10 minutes                Makes about 425 ml (14½ fl oz)
+ 1 hour cooking

*300 ml (½ pint) milk*

*half a vanilla pod, split in two*

*4 egg yolks*

*65 g (2½ oz) vanilla caster sugar (page 8)*

*25 g (1 oz) plain flour*

*a pinch of salt*

*This is not only useful as a filling for tarts and pastries but can also be the basis for soufflés.*

Bring the milk, the salt and the vanilla pod to boiling point. Remove from the heat, cover, and leave for 15 minutes to infuse. Whisk the egg yolks and sugar until thick and then whisk in the sifted flour. Remove the pod from the milk (dry it and put it with sugar for vanilla sugar) and bring the milk back to the boil. Whisk the milk into the egg mixture, pour back into the pan and continue to stir over a low heat until the mixture thickens. Simmer for 2–3 minutes, stirring, to ensure that the flour loses its uncooked taste. Place a piece of cling film over the surface to prevent a skin forming. Refrigerate when cool and use within two days.

*Chocolate Crème Patissiere:* follow the above recipe omitting the vanilla pod and using one less egg yolk. After stirring for 2–3 minutes, stir in 50 g (2 oz) of chopped plain chocolate.

## PRALINE

Preparation time: 15 minutes + 1 hour cooling      Makes 300 g (10 oz)

*oil for greasing*

*125 g (4 oz) unblanched almonds*

*125 g (4 oz) granulated sugar*

Oil a marble surface or baking sheet. Place the nuts and sugar in a small heavy-bottomed saucepan. Set over a low heat until the sugar starts to melt. Continue cooking, stirring occasionally until the sugar goes a dark brown. The sugar may go lumpy at first but it will dissolve as it colours. When the mixture is a good caramel colour, pour it quickly on to the prepared surface. Leave until it is quite cold and hard and then grind it with a rolling pin, rotary cheese grater or processor.

## CHOCOLATE BUTTER CREAM

Preparation time: 15 minutes      Will frost a 20 cm (8-inch) layered cake

*100 g (3½ oz) plain chocolate*

*125 g (4 oz) granulated sugar*

*100 ml (3½ fl oz) water*

*3 egg yolks*

*250 g (8 oz) unsalted butter, softened*

*a pinch of salt*

*Butter cream will keep in the refrigerator for several days and can also be frozen.*

Melt the chocolate with the salt in the top of a double saucepan (page 10) and set aside. Using a heavy-bottomed saucepan, dissolve the sugar in the water over low heat. Raise the heat and boil the syrup until it reaches 110°C/225°F on a sugar thermometer. Whisk the egg yolks in a bowl and gradually pour in the hot syrup, whisking constantly, until the mixture is thick and cool. Stir in the melted chocolate. Cream the butter until it is very soft and smooth; then gradually beat it into the chocolate mixture, ensuring that the mixture is well combined.

# ROCKY ROAD

| Preparation time: 10 minutes + 1½ hours setting | Makes about 625 g (1¼ lb) |

*500 g (1 lb) milk chocolate, broken into small pieces*

*12 marshmallows, diced*

*75 g (3 oz) walnuts, pecans or almonds or a mixture of nuts, chopped roughly*

*Children love this popular American candy made with milk chocolate, marshmallows and nuts. The bumpy surface explains the name.*

Line a baking sheet approximately 15 × 25 cm (6 × 10 inches) with baking parchment. Melt the chocolate in the top of a double saucepan (page 10). When the chocolate has melted stir in the marshmallows and nuts, and pour the mixture into the prepared tin. With an oiled palette knife smooth over the surface covering any nuts and marshmallows with the chocolate. Leave it to set for 1–1½ hours in the fridge before breaking it into bite-size pieces.

*Banana Rocky Road:* substitute 125 g (4 oz) of dried banana chips for the marshmallows and nuts and follow the above recipe.

*Armagnac Prune Bonbons*

_Rocky Road_

_Chocolate Truffles_

_White Chocolate Truffles_

89

# ARMAGNAC PRUNE BONBONS

Preparation and cooking time: 50 minutes
+ 5 days soaking + 25 hours chilling

Makes 875 g (1¾ lb)

### For the bonbons:

250 g (8 oz) soft prunes

125 ml (4 fl oz) Armagnac

275 g (9 oz) plain chocolate, cut into small pieces

250 ml (8 fl oz) double cream

50 g (2 oz) unsalted butter, cut into small pieces

### To coat the bonbons:

450 g (15 oz) plain chocolate, cut into small pieces

2 tablespoons sunflower or groundnut oil

a few walnut pieces for decoration

*These amazingly scrumptious sweets make great gifts and will dazzle your guests. A plain chocolate covering hides a delectable bonbon flavoured with Armagnac-soaked prunes.*

For the bonbons: soak the prunes in the Armagnac, covered, for five days. Place the chocolate, cream and butter in the top of a double saucepan set over barely simmering water and stir until the mixture is smooth. Take the mixture off the heat and leave it to cool. Strain the prunes, reserving any liquid. Stone and cut the prunes into pea-size pieces. Stir the prunes into the chocolate cream and add 2 tablespoons of the soaking liquid. Cover and refrigerate the chocolate for 24 hours.

Line a baking sheet with baking parchment. Spoon out teaspoons of the chocolate mixture and form it into balls by rolling it between your palms. Place the bonbons on the baking sheet and refrigerate for 1 hour, or up to 24 before coating.

To coat the bonbons: melt the chocolate carefully (page 10). Stir in the oil and allow the chocolate to drop to a temperature of 40–42°C/ 90–95°F. Work with a few chocolates at a time, and keep the others refrigerated. Drop a chocolate into the coating and turn it with a fork to coat all over. Lift it out with a fork, and scrape the bottom of the fork against the edge of the pan to remove any excess chocolate. Slide the chocolate on to a baking sheet lined with baking parchment. Place a small piece of walnut on top of each chocolate before it sets. Keep the bonbons refrigerated and eat them within ten days.

# CHOCOLATE TRUFFLES

Preparation time: 45 minutes + 24 hours cooling    Makes 625 g (1¼ lb)

### For the truffles:

200 ml (7 fl oz) single cream

25 g (1 oz) butter

500 g (1 lb) plain chocolate, chopped

2 tablespoons rum, Cognac or liqueur of your choice

25 g (1 oz) Praline (page 87) optional

### To coat the truffles:

4 tablespoons cocoa powder

1 tablespoon icing sugar

chocolate vermicelli

Praline

*I like home-made chocolate truffles quite small and quite alcoholic to serve with after-dinner coffee.*

Using a heavy-bottomed saucepan, heat the cream and the butter until they reach a rolling boil. Remove the mixture from the heat and stir in the chocolate. When it has melted add the liqueur. Pour the chocolate mixture into a shallow tin lined with baking parchment and spread out with a palette knife. Leave it in a cool place, uncovered, for 24 hours.

Pull off small pieces and roll them into balls in the palms of your hands. Add the Praline to some of the truffles if desired.

To coat the truffles: sift the cocoa and icing sugar together on to a square of baking parchment and roll the truffles either in this or in the vermicelli or Praline. You can use a different coating for different flavours. Keep the truffles refrigerated in a covered container layered with baking parchment.

# WHITE CHOCOLATE TRUFFLES

Preparation time: 10 minutes + 2 hours chilling         Makes about 30

175 g (6 oz) white chocolate, chopped

65 g (2½ oz) unsalted butter, cut into pieces

3 tablespoons double cream

1 teaspoon orange liqueur

a pinch of salt

*White chocolate is very much in vogue. These meltingly good truffles make a stunning contrast when arranged with dark truffles.*

Place the chocolate, butter, cream and salt in the top of a double saucepan set over barely simmering water and stir until the mixture is smooth. Remove the mixture from the heat and add the liqueur. Cover and refrigerate it until firm, about 2 hours. Pull off marble-size pieces and roll them in the palms of your hands to shape them into balls. If the mixture becomes difficult to handle, return to the refrigerator and chill further. Keep the truffles refrigerated in a covered container layered with baking parchment.

## HOT FUDGE SAUCE

Preparation time: 10 minutes                    Makes 300 ml (½ pint)

125 ml (4 fl oz) whipping cream

25 g (1 oz) unsalted butter

40 g (1½ oz) cocoa, sifted

50 g (2 oz) caster sugar

50 g (2 oz) soft dark brown sugar

a pinch of salt

Place all the ingredients in a heavy saucepan and stir over a low heat until the mixture is smooth. Add more sugar if it seems too bitter for your taste.

## MARMALADE SAUCE

Preparation time: 10 minutes                    Makes 300 ml (½ pint)

125 g (4 oz) chunky marmalade

juice of half a lemon

2–3 tablespoons water

2 tablespoons orange liqueur

Bring the first three ingredients to the boil. Remove the sauce from the heat and stir in the liqueur. You can serve the sauce hot or cold. If it is to be served hot, omit the water.

## PISTACHIO SAUCE

Preparation and cooking time: 1 hour            Makes 450 ml (¾ pint)

75 g (3 oz) shelled pistachio nuts

25 g (1 oz) blanched almonds

75 g (3 oz) vanilla caster sugar (page 8)

300 ml (½ pint) milk

3 egg yolks

1–2 drops of green food colouring (optional)

*Pistachio Sauce*
*Hot Fudge Sauce*
*Marmalade Sauce* ➤

Blanch the pistachio nuts in boiling water for 1 minute. Drain, then rub them between a tea cloth to remove some of the skins. Blend or process the pistachios and almonds with a few tablespoons of the sugar. Add a few tablespoons of milk and process to a smooth paste. Heat the milk with the nut paste to just below boiling point. Cover and leave to infuse for 15 minutes. Reheat the milk again to below boiling point. Whisk the egg yolks with the remaining sugar, and then whisk in the hot milk. Return the mixture to the pan and cook it over a very low heat, stirring with a wooden spoon, until the custard slightly thickens. Do not allow it to boil or it will curdle. Strain the sauce into a bowl and

when cool add the colouring if used. You might want to add a heaped tablespoon of the pistachio purée to give texture to the sauce. When cool, cover and refrigerate. The sauce will keep refrigerated for three days.

## BITTER CHOCOLATE SAUCE

Preparation and cooking time: 15 minutes          Makes 300 ml (½ pint)

*100 g (3½ oz) bitter dessert chocolate*

*25 g (1 oz) butter*

*5 tablespoons water*

*1 tablespoon rum or brandy*

Melt the first three ingredients together in a small heavy–bottomed saucepan over a gentle heat, stirring constantly. Do not allow it to boil. Stir in the alcohol and serve it warm or cold.
   *Chocolate Mint Sauce:* omit the alcohol and add a few drops of oil of peppermint.
   *Rum Raisin Sauce:* soak some raisins in rum for several hours and add to the chocolate sauce.
   *Note:* both variations can be made using the Chocolate Sauce below.

## CHOCOLATE SAUCE

Preparation and cooking time: 15 minutes          Makes 450 ml (¾ pint)

*50 g (2 oz) cocoa*

*125 g (4 oz) vanilla caster sugar (page 8)*

*250 ml (8 fl oz) cold water*

*25 g (1 oz) unsalted butter*

*a pinch of salt*

*This alternative sauce is made with cocoa.*

Simmer the cocoa, vanilla caster sugar, cold water and salt together, stirring for 3 minutes. Stir in the butter, bring to a simmer again, adding a little more water if necessary to make a pouring consistency, and serve warm or cold.
*Note:* see the above recipe for variations.

## CHOCOLATE GANACHE

Preparation time: 20 minutes          23 cm (9-inch) layered cake

*200 g (7 oz) plain chocolate*

*125 ml (4 fl oz) milk*

*300 ml (½ pint) double cream*

*A gorgeous chocolate cream mousse frosting.*

Melt the chocolate (page 10). Using a small saucepan, bring the milk to the boil and immediately pour it over the chocolate, whisking until the mixture is smooth. Leave it to cool. Whip the cream to soft peaks and then fold it in the chocolate cream.

# INDEX TO RECIPES

Design and layout: Ken Vail Graphic Design
Photography: Andrew Whittuck
Stylist: Bobby Baker
Food preparation for photography: Jane Suthering
Illustrations: Mandy Doyle
Typesetting: Westholme Graphics
Printed and bound by Balding & Mansell Ltd,
Wisbech, Cambs